Low Waste Kitchen

Low Waste Kitchen

ALESSANDRO VITALE
aka Spicy Moustache

Radical recipes for sustainable living

Contents

Introduction   *6*

Leafy Greens   *16*

Roots and Shoots   *30*

Grains and Pulses   *54*

Nuts and Seeds   *74*

Flowers   *92*

Fruit   *110*

Herbs   *154*

Flour-Based Recipes   *160*

Home Remedies   *176*

Index   *186*

Acknowledgments   *191*

Welcome to the Low Waste Kitchen

I'm Alessandro Vitale, also known as Spicy Moustache. I might not fit the typical image of someone who tends to a productive garden and preserves every part of every fruit and vegetable to prevent waste—but as they say, never judge a book by its cover.

Along with my partner Iasmina, who has grown alongside me every step of the way, I've committed to a low-waste approach to life. Iasmina and I started sharing our tips and recipes on social media during the pandemic—but in truth, it all started much earlier, during my childhood.

My grandparents inspired me to preserve their values and traditions. They never actually spoke about the idea of "zero waste"—this concept, though it began to gain significance in the 1970s, didn't become widely recognized in the way it is today until the 1990s. For my grandparents, using every part of their fruits and vegetables wasn't just a trend but a way of life. They cherished each ingredient, finding creative ways to give new life to what would otherwise be discarded—whether in the garden or the kitchen—harvesting zucchini stems, dandelion leaves, and green tomatoes to transform them into delicious, nourishing, and plant-based food. This philosophy always stayed with me, and it evolved as Iasmina and I absorbed the rich cultures and traditions of our ancestors—from Brazil, Italy, the Balkans, and Germany—and learned from every single culture we encountered during our travels around the world. Each place, each tradition, added a layer of wisdom to the way we cook and live sustainably today.

This book is not just a tribute to my grandparents, a way to preserve their legacy; it is also an invitation to younger generations to make lifestyle changes and care for the environment. By cooking simply with plants, preferably organic or homegrown, and making the best use of every last scrap, we can make a real difference. It's a cause that transcends borders and emphasizes that every small action matters. After all, we don't need thousands of people doing it perfectly; we need millions of people doing it imperfectly.

"Zero-waste living" is a concept that strives to eliminate as much waste as possible by redesigning resource use and consumption. However, the reality for many people is that the idea of a completely waste-free life can feel overwhelming or impractical. This is where "low-waste living" comes in. By living in this way, we focus on reducing waste wherever we can, while acknowledging that perfect solutions might not always be accessible. It's about making small, manageable changes that fit your lifestyle.

In this book, I'll guide you through the principles of low-waste living, specifically in the kitchen. All the recipes in this book are completely plant-based and can be made with homegrown produce and simple pantry ingredients. You'll find practical solutions for everything from storing food to make it last longer to maximizing the use of every ingredient and reducing food waste. Whether you have a large kitchen or a tiny corner for your culinary adventures, these strategies can be adapted to suit your needs.

Ultimately, this book is here to show you that creating less waste doesn't mean drastically changing your life overnight. It's about making thoughtful, achievable adjustments and building habits that benefit both you and the planet.

Work with what you have

The first thing I want to make clear is that you don't need to go out and buy a lot of new items to transform your kitchen into a low-waste haven. After all, we're trying to reduce consumption and avoid waste. Begin where you are; you'll probably find that you have a lot of what you need already.

The same applies if you're reading this book and a recipe calls for a particular-sized pan or baking sheet. You don't need to go and buy one; just use what you have, adjust the quantities or timings if needed, and enjoy your low-waste goodness.

Repurposing jars

Jars are among the most useful items in a low-waste kitchen. They're easy to clean, they make great storage, and you can see what's inside them at a glance. But there's no need to go out and buy brand-new mason jars. You can just reuse the jars that are already in your kitchen. Once a jar is empty, clean the jar and its lid thoroughly in hot, soapy water. Let the jar soak in the warm water for a while; this will help loosen the label. If the label is stubbornly stuck on, you can use a little olive oil to help

Sterilizing jars

Sometimes my recipes call for sterilized jars. This can sound very serious, but it's really simple. There are two easy methods for sterilizing jars. One uses a large pan, and one uses an oven.

Method 1: Boil

» Wash your jars thoroughly with hot, soapy water, then rinse. Place the jars upright in a large saucepan, then pour over enough water to completely cover. Bring to a boil, then boil for 10 minutes. Turn off the heat and let the jars cool in the water until they're safe to touch. For crystal-clear jars, add a splash of white vinegar to the water.

Method 2: Oven

» Wash your jars thoroughly with hot, soapy water, then rinse. Place them on a baking sheet and transfer to an oven preheated to 275°F (140°C). Leave them in the oven for about 10 minutes until completely dry, then let cool. (Note: don't use this method for jars with rubber seals.)

remove it. Let the jar dry completely, then use it to store whatever you like. You can use masking tape and a pen to make your own labels.

Food storage

One of the best ways to avoid food waste is to store your food carefully and correctly. Adopting the right storage methods will make your food last longer, ensuring you get as much use out of it as possible.

Best by when?

A lot of supermarket foods are marked with a "Best by" date, but this isn't the same as a "Use by" date; it might mean that the item is a little less fresh, but it doesn't automatically mean it isn't OK to eat. Particularly when it comes to things like fruits and vegetables, pay attention to the items themselves and learn to judge when they need to be used up. It's also a really good idea to arrange your refrigerator or pantry with the foods that have a shorter shelf life near the front, so you remember to use them first. And be creative—for example, if your leaves are looking a little too wilted to enjoy in a salad, they could still be blended up into a delicious smoothie or transformed into a nutritious soup.

Pantry
Dried goods

Store dried goods like pasta, pulses, flour, rice, and grains in jars in your pantry. This will help them last longer and also means you can see at a glance what each jar contains and how much is left. Store spices and vegetable skin powders (see p34) in small labeled jars.

Fruit

For fruits that are best stored at room temperature, arrange them in bowls. It is best to use different bowls for different fruits as they will ripen at different speeds.

Tomatoes

To make tomatoes last longer, line a container with a clean kitchen towel. Arrange the tomatoes in the container stem-side down, then cover with another towel. Storing them upside down helps them stay fresher longer.

Potatoes

Store potatoes in a paper or mesh bag and keep in a cool, dark place to prevent sprouting. Don't wash your potatoes until you're ready to use them, as the soil can help preserve them for longer.

Onions and garlic

Store these in a paper bag in a cool, dark place. I like to put the paper bag in a mesh bag and hang it up to ensure they are well ventilated.

Refrigerator
Stem vegetables

Trim the ends of stem vegetables like asparagus, kale, celery, and green onions (keep the trimmings to make your own vegetable stock). Fill a jar with 1–2in (2.5–5cm) water and immerse the ends of the trimmed vegetables in the water, then place the jar in the refrigerator. Refresh the water every couple of days to keep them fresh.

Root vegetables

Vegetables like carrots, radishes, and parsnips can be chopped into large chunks and then placed in a jar, covered with water, and refrigerated.

Leafy green vegetables

These can be laid in a container lined with a clean, dry kitchen towel or paper towel, then covered with a wax wrap (see below). The towel will absorb excess moisture and ensure they stay crisp.

Herbs

To help herbs stay fresh, flavorful, and colorful, wrap them lightly in a damp cloth and place in an airtight container in the refrigerator.

Berries

Remove any green parts or stems, then soak your berries in a bowl of water with a dash of vinegar. Gently dry with a clean towel, then transfer to an airtight container and store in the refrigerator.

~~~~~~~~~~

Wrapping food
Wrapping food can be one of those situations where a lot of waste occurs, as people often wrap leftovers using single-use plastics like plastic wrap. Avoid this as much as you can by using food storage containers with lids. If you do need to use plastic wrap (and sometimes it is necessary), always use a biodegradable, compostable brand.

DIY wax wraps
I like to use wax wraps in my kitchen. These are very popular and easy to buy online and in stores, but did you know you can make your own?

» Take some clean old cloth (for example, from old T-shirts or aprons) and cut it into squares of the appropriate size. Lay out the cloth squares on a heatproof surface lined with parchment paper. Melt soy wax pellets (or grated soy wax) over a low heat (or use beeswax if you prefer), then use a brush to lightly brush it over the fabric. Cover with another sheet of parchment paper, then briefly iron with the iron on a low setting. There you have it—your own homemade wax wraps.

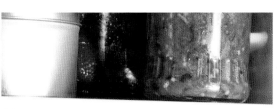

Freezer

Most cooked and fresh foods are suitable for freezing, and frozen foods can last for months if stored correctly, so this is a great way to avoid food waste. Whole fresh fruits and vegetables can be easily frozen to use in dishes later in the year—but remember, those with a high water content (strawberries, for instance) will change in texture when frozen (but will still be fine for cooking with, once defrosted). Store food in freezer-proof containers, or well wrapped in layers of biodegradable plastic wrap and foil. Defrost thoroughly in the fridge and ensure the food is completely cooked through when reheating. Alongside preservation methods like pickling, using your freezer well means you can enjoy your favorite foods even when they're not in season.

Low-waste shopping

As you probably know, I am a keen gardener, and I love to use the produce I grow in my kitchen. If you have any outside space at all, I encourage you to do the same, as there is no greater satisfaction than eating a meal made with ingredients you have nurtured, grown, and harvested yourself.

Of course, this is not an option for everyone, but there are plenty of other ways to adopt a low-waste approach to your groceries.

Farmers' markets

I love to visit a farmers' market and see all the fantastic, colorful produce. It's a great way to get inspiration for what to cook, and it can help you keep in touch with what's in season. Get to know the stallholders and take your time choosing the right fruits and vegetables for you—and remember to ask if they have any cutoffs or trimmings (for example, so you can make Carrot-Top Pesto; see page 42). So that you can enjoy every part of your fruits and vegetables, including the peel and skin, certified organic produce is best. Bring along your own mesh vegetable bags and reusable carrier bags for bringing home your bounty.

Refill or low-waste stores

If you're lucky enough to have a refill or low-waste store in your neighborhood, I really recommend you use it. Not only will it enable you to drastically cut your own household waste, but it's also important to use these facilities to ensure we don't lose them. People sometimes think that these stores are expensive, but they can actually be really cost-effective, as you're buying only as much as you need, so you don't waste anything. Bring along your own containers and take part in the low-waste revolution.

Of course, not everyone has these resources available to them, but wherever you shop, always try to choose local, seasonal, and organic produce. Not only will you be supporting your local economy and helping the environment, but you'll also be looking after your own health. Choosing organic foods that are grown free of pesticides is important for a low-waste lifestyle, as we want to make use of every part of the plant, including the peels and skins.

Be a creative cook

This is my last point, but it's a really important one. I want these recipes to be an inspiring starting point, not a list of rules for you to follow. If I've used an ingredient you don't have or don't like, then swap it out for something else. Experiment with the seasonings and flavors in every dish, and see what works best for you. Sometimes I've suggested certain herbs or spices, but you could try something else and discover your new favorite flavor combination. The ingredients, quantities, and methods in this book are guidelines only—don't let them restrict you. The low-waste kitchen is a place to be creative, playful, and a little bit rebellious. So come on— let's have some fun with it!

Leafy
Greens

Spinach	Spinach and Ricotta Cannelloni Crêpes	**18**
Nettles	Nettle Risotto	**19**
Lettuce	Lettuce and Potato Soup	**20**
	Stuffed Lettuce Leaves	**22**
Cabbage	Red Cabbage Soup	**23**
	Sarmale de Post (Stuffed Cabbage Rolls)	**24**
	Kimchi	**29**

Spinach and Ricotta Cannelloni Crêpes

This dish reminds me of family meals on a Sunday. It's hearty and delicious, and my mom used to make it for any special occasion. I tested many combinations to replicate the same flavors my mom used to create, and I came up with this absolutely delicious dish.

Serves 4–6
Prep time 20 minutes
Cooking time 50 minutes

Ingredients

2 cups (270g) all-purpose flour

2 cups (450ml) soy milk

3 tbsp olive oil or vegetable oil, plus extra for cooking

3 tbsp granulated sugar

salt and freshly ground black pepper

For the ricotta filling

2 tbsp olive oil

1 onion, finely chopped

4 garlic cloves, finely chopped

7oz (200g) spinach

14oz (400g) Plant-Based Ricotta (see p164)

For the béchamel sauce

3 tbsp plant-based butter

3 tbsp all-purpose flour

2 cups (450ml) soy milk

⅓ tsp ground nutmeg

For the topping

1 x 15oz (425g) can tomato purée

handful of grated plant-based cheese

Prepare the crêpes In a mixing bowl, combine the flour, soy milk, oil, sugar, and a pinch of salt. Whisk until smooth and free of lumps. Heat a small amount of oil in a nonstick skillet over medium heat. Pour about 4 tablespoons of the batter into the pan. Cook for 1–2 minutes until the edges start to lift and the bottom is lightly golden, then flip and cook on the other side for 1 minute. Transfer to a plate and repeat until all the batter is used up. Set aside.

Make the ricotta filling Heat the oil in a large skillet over medium heat. Add the onion and sauté for 5 minutes until translucent, then add the garlic and sauté for another minute. Stir in the spinach and cook for 3 minutes until wilted. Remove from the heat and mix in the ricotta. Season, then set aside.

Prepare the béchamel sauce Melt the butter in a small saucepan over medium heat. Once melted, stir in the flour and cook, whisking constantly, for 1–2 minutes to form a roux. Gradually add the soy milk, whisking all the time to ensure the mixture remains smooth. Cook for about 5 minutes until it thickens, stirring. Season with salt, pepper, and nutmeg. Remove from heat and set aside.

Preheat the oven Preheat the oven to 400°F (200°C).

Assemble Lay a crêpe on a clean surface. Spoon 2–3 tablespoons of the ricotta filling along one edge of the crêpe. Tightly roll up the crêpe, then place it seam-side down in a large baking dish. Repeat with the remaining crêpes and filling. Pour the tomato purée evenly over the crêpes, then drizzle the béchamel sauce on top. Sprinkle over the plant-based cheese.

Bake Cover the baking dish with foil and bake for 25 minutes, then remove the foil and bake for an additional 10 minutes, or until golden and bubbling.

Serve Remove from the oven and let it cool for a few minutes before serving.

Storage Store leftovers in an airtight container in the refrigerator for up to 3 days.

Nettle Risotto

I used to think nettles were a nightmare when I cycled around the local river in Italy, mainly because I fell into a bush of them when I was a kid, and I still remember the excruciating pain of the stings all over my body. However, over the years, I've started appreciating the medicinal and culinary uses of this plant. You can use nettle leaves to make pasta, gnocchi, and many more things, but my favorite way to use them is in this risotto. Always wear gloves when picking nettles.

Serves 4–6
Prep time 15 minutes
Cooking time 30 minutes

Ingredients

9oz (250g) nettle leaves, stems removed

3 tbsp olive oil, plus extra to serve

1 onion, finely diced

3 garlic cloves, finely chopped

1⅔ cup (300g) risotto rice

6½ tbsp (100ml) white wine

6 cups (1.4 liters) vegetable stock (homemade or made using 1–2 stock cubes)

1 tsp salt, or to taste

⅓ tsp freshly ground black pepper, plus extra to serve

2–3 tbsp plant-based cream cheese

Prepare the nettles Bring a large pot of water to a boil. Add the nettle leaves to the boiling water and blanch for 1–2 minutes. This will remove their sting. Drain and immediately transfer to a bowl of iced water to stop the cooking process. Once cooled, drain again, then roughly chop the nettle leaves. Set aside.

Sauté the aromatics Heat the olive oil in a large pan over medium heat. Add the onion and sauté for about 5 minutes until it becomes translucent, then stir in the chopped garlic and cook for another minute until fragrant.

Toast the rice Add the rice and cook for 2–3 minutes until lightly toasted.

Deglaze with wine Pour in the white wine and stir constantly until it is mostly absorbed by the rice.

Cook the risotto Begin adding the vegetable stock, a ladleful at a time. Stir frequently, allowing the rice to absorb most of the stock before adding more. Continue this process, adding the stock a little at a time, until the rice is creamy and al dente. This should take 18–20 minutes.

Add the nettles Stir in the chopped nettles, along with the salt and black pepper. Cook for an additional 2–3 minutes until the nettles are heated through.

Finish and serve Remove from the heat and stir in the plant-based cream cheese. Finish with a drizzle of olive oil and some black pepper, and serve.

Storage Store leftovers in an airtight container in the refrigerator for up to 3 days. Reheat gently with a splash of vegetable stock to restore the creamy texture.

Lettuce and Potato Soup

Lettuce in soup? Absolutely! This dish is quite popular in the Balkan area, where soup is a must, even in summertime. It's a brilliant way to use up that head of lettuce sitting at the back of the fridge, transforming it into a smooth, velvety soup that's both nutritious and satisfying, with the heartiness of potatoes and a smoky hint of paprika. This soup perfectly embodies the essence of homemade comfort food, taking you on a delightful journey from simple ingredients to a bowlful of coziness. It's proof that even the most overlooked veggies can become the stars of the show.

Serves 4–6

Prep time 15 minutes

Cooking time 50 minutes

Ingredients

3 tbsp olive oil

1 large onion, finely chopped

3 garlic cloves, minced

2 medium potatoes, diced

1 tsp smoked paprika

6 cups (1.4 liters) water

1 romaine or iceberg lettuce, chopped

2 green onions, chopped

handful of dill, chopped

salt and freshly ground black pepper

plant-based sour cream, to serve

Sauté the aromatics Heat the olive oil in a large saucepan over medium heat. Add the onion and garlic, and sauté for 5-10 minutes until softened and aromatic.

Add the potatoes and smoked paprika Stir in the potatoes and smoked paprika, ensuring the potatoes are well coated in the spice.

Season and simmer Season with salt and black pepper to taste. Pour in the water and bring to a boil, then reduce the heat to low and let it simmer for about 20-25 minutes until the potatoes are tender.

Add the greens Add the chopped lettuce, green onions, and dill to the pan, and simmer for another 5-7 minutes until the greens are infused with flavor. Taste and adjust the seasoning if needed.

Serve Ladle the soup into bowls and swirl in a little plant-based sour cream to serve.

Storage Store any leftover soup in an airtight container in the refrigerator for up to 3 days.

Stuffed Lettuce Leaves

Stuffed lettuce leaves are my go-to when I want a meal that's fresh, flavorful, and fuss-free. It's a creative way to pack a variety of textures and tastes into every bite, using lettuce as a crisp, edible container. This recipe is all about versatility and making the most of what you have on hand, turning simple ingredients into a vibrant, satisfying meal.

Serves 4

Prep time 15 minutes

Ingredients

8-10 large lettuce leaves (such as iceberg or romaine), washed and patted dry

2 cups (370g) cooked jasmine or basmati rice

⅔ cup (140g) canned sweet corn

1 large tomato, diced

1 ripe avocado, sliced

finely chopped chives, to serve

For the plant-based garlic cream

1 cup (240ml) plant-based cream

2 garlic cloves, minced

1 tbsp nutritional yeast

1 tbsp lemon juice

salt and freshly ground black pepper

Fill the lettuce leaves Lay out the lettuce leaves on a flat surface. Place a generous scoop of cooked rice in the center of each lettuce leaf. Sprinkle over the sweet corn and tomato, then arrange the avocado slices on top.

Prepare the plant-based garlic cream In a bowl, whisk together the plant-based cream, minced garlic, nutritional yeast, and lemon juice, and season to taste with salt and pepper.

Drizzle, sprinkle, and serve Drizzle the plant-based garlic cream over the stuffed lettuce wraps, then sprinkle the chives on top for an extra burst of flavor. Serve the lettuce wraps open-faced and bite into the delicious layers.

Storage Best eaten immediately to maintain freshness. Store any leftover plant-based garlic cream in an airtight container in the refrigerator for up to a week.

Red Cabbage Soup

Growing cabbages in the UK can be challenging because the weather conditions attract slugs and snails, which can easily damage the plant at early/late stages. However, after years of testing and lots of failures, I managed to successfully grow a variety of different cabbages—which ultimately left us with too many to process and eat in a short amount of time. This is when Iasmina had the brilliant idea of adding a twist to a traditional Romanian recipe, creating this incredibly delicious dish.

Serves 4–6

Prep time 15 minutes

Cooking time 40 minutes

Ingredients

3½ tbsp olive oil, plus extra to serve

1 red onion, finely chopped

1 celery stick, chopped

4 garlic cloves, minced

1 apple, peeled, cored, and chopped

1¾lb (800g) red cabbage, shredded

2 bay leaves

1 x 14oz (400g) can butter beans, drained and rinsed

1 vegetable stock cube

2¾ cup (1.5 liters) water (or up to 8½ cups/2 liters for thinner consistency)

1 tbsp balsamic vinegar

½ tsp salt

freshly ground black pepper

To serve

handful of microgreens

plant-based sour cream

Sauté the vegetables Heat the olive oil in a large pot over medium heat. Add the red onion, celery, and garlic, and sauté for about 5 minutes until the onion is soft and translucent. Add the chopped apple and cook for another 3 minutes, stirring occasionally.

Cook the soup Stir in the shredded red cabbage and cook for about 5 minutes until it starts to soften. Add the bay leaves, drained butter beans, and vegetable stock cube, then pour the water. Bring the mixture to a boil, then reduce the heat to a simmer, and cook for 25–30 minutes, or until the cabbage is tender.

Season and blend Fish out and discard the bay leaves, then stir in the balsamic vinegar and salt. Season with black pepper to taste. For a smoother consistency, blend the soup using an immersion blender until the desired texture is achieved. You can blend it completely for a creamy soup, or leave some chunks if you like a bit more texture.

Serve Ladle the soup into bowls, and serve with a dollop of plant-based sour cream, a sprinkle of microgreens, and a drizzle of olive oil.

Storage Store leftovers in an airtight container in the refrigerator for up to 3 days. This soup can also be frozen for up to 2 months.

Sarmale de Post (Stuffed Cabbage Rolls)

I just love sarmale! I tried this recipe for the first time when visiting Timișoara in Romania with Iasmina. It's extremely easy to make and a staple food in traditional Romanian and Eastern European cuisine. Think about it as the best cozy food for a cold day in winter—though I could honestly eat it every single day. You can find whole fermented cabbages or fermented cabbage leaves in Eastern European grocery stores.

Makes 15–20 rolls

Prep time 20 minutes, plus cooling

Cooking time 30-35 minutes

Ingredients

1 tbsp olive oil

3 onions, chopped

3 garlic cloves, minced

1 celery stick, finely chopped

9oz (250g) mushrooms, diced

1 tbsp chopped dill

1 tbsp chopped flat-leaf parsley

1 tsp sweet paprika

1½ cups (285g) round-grain rice (short-grain or long-grain rice will also work)

2 store-bought medium fermented cabbages, or 15–20 store-bought fermented cabbage leaves, plus extra to line the dish

14-21 oz (400-600g) tomato purée

2-3 bay leaves

salt and freshly ground black pepper

plant-based sour cream, to serve

fresh dill, to serve

Prepare the filling Heat the olive oil in a saucepan over medium heat. Add the onions, garlic, celery, and mushrooms, and sauté for 5-10 minutes until softened. Add the dill, parsley, and sweet paprika, and season with salt and pepper to taste. Stir in the rice and cook for 1-2 minutes to toast it lightly until golden. Set aside to cool.

Prepare the cabbage leaves Carefully separate the cabbage leaves, trying to keep them whole. If they are too salty, rinse them with water.

Stuff the leaves Place a spoonful of the cooled filling in the center of each cabbage leaf. Fold in the sides and roll up the leaf to enclose the filling.

Layer the sarmale Line the base of a large, deep saucepan with some spare cabbage leaves to prevent sticking, then lay the rolls in the pan, placing them next to each other and packing them in tightly. Chop any extra cabbage leaves and place them on top of the rolls, then pour over the tomato purée, and add the bay leaves. Pour over enough water to just cover the rolls.

Cook Bring to a boil, then reduce the heat to low. Cover and simmer for 20-25 minutes.

Enjoy Serve the sarmale warm with a dollop of plant-based sour cream and a sprinkling of dill, if you like.

Storage Store any leftover sarmale in the refrigerator in an airtight container. They should keep well for up to 3-4 days. Reheat before serving. They will also freeze for up to 3 months—defrost fully before reheating.

Note
» Try adding carrots, peas, legumes, or plant-based meat substitutes to your filling.

Prepare the filling

Prepare the leaves

Stuff the leaves

Roll the leaves

26

Prepare the cabbages

Prepare the kimchi

Ferment

Kimchi

This Korean staple isn't just a side dish; it's a culinary rock star! Bursting with bold flavors and a spicy kick, kimchi is all about bringing the heat and health to your meals. It's a fermented fiesta, packed with probiotics that do wonders for your gut health. But wait, there's more—kimchi is incredibly versatile. Use it in a stew, mix it with white rice, or pile it on top of your favorite plant-based burger. It's even amazing straight out of the jar! And the best part? You can easily make it at home and tweak the spice levels to your liking. It's a long process, so I think it's worth making a big batch each time, but if you prefer, you can scale down this recipe to make a smaller quantity.

Makes about 7–8lb (3–4kg)

Prep time 15–20 minutes, plus resting time

Fermentation time 2 days

Ingredients

6lb (2.7kg) napa cabbages (about 4 medium cabbages)
⅓ cup (72g) kosher salt

For the "porridge"

2 tbsp glutinous rice flour
2 cups (475ml) water
2 tbsp Demerara sugar (or any brown or white sugar)

For the seasoning paste

24 garlic cloves, minced
2 tsp minced ginger
1 onion, very finely chopped
½ cup (120ml) soy sauce
2 cups (190g) hot pepper flakes (gochugaru)
1 bunch (about 8-10) radishes, chopped into matchsticks
5 medium carrots, chopped into matchsticks
7–8 green onions, chopped
handful of Asian chives (buchu), chopped (regular chives can also be used)

Equipment

enough sterilized jars or containers to hold 7lb (3.6kg) of kimchi

- -

Prepare the cabbages Halve each cabbage lengthwise and place on a plate or in a bowl. Sprinkle the salt generously over and between the leaves as shown. Let sit for 2 hours, turning every 30 minutes.

Make the "porridge" Meanwhile, in a saucepan, combine the rice flour with the water and place over medium heat. Cook until it bubbles, then add the sugar and stir until the mixture thickens. Set aside to cool.

Make the seasoning paste and mix with the veggies In a bowl, mix together the garlic, ginger, onion, soy sauce, and pepper flakes. Add the cooled porridge and stir well to combine. Add the radishes, carrots, green onions, and chives, and stir to coat.

Rinse the cabbage After the salting time is up, rinse and drain the cabbages.

Prepare the kimchi Apply the vegetable and seasoning mixture between each cabbage leaf.

Ferment Transfer the cabbages into the prepared jars, pressing them down with your fist. Cover and let ferment at room temperature for 2 days.

Storage Once the fermentation time is up, the kimchi is ready to eat. It will keep in the refrigerator for several months and will continue to ferment, with its flavor enhancing over time.

Roots
and
Shoots

Ferments and Powders	Lacto-Fermented Vegetables	32
	Vegetable Skin Powders	34
Alliums	Upside-Down Onion Tart	38
	Confit Garlic with Garden Herbs	39
Carrots	Crispy Potato and Carrot Skin Snacks	40
	Fresh Carrot Juice	40
	Carrot-Top Pesto	42
	Carrot Turkish Truffles	42
	Carrot Cupcakes	43
Ginger	Ginger Shot	44
	Curry Powder Mix	44
	Ginger Bug	44
Potatoes	Stuffed Flatbread	47
	Potato Noodles	48
	Vegan Arrabbiata Sauce	49
	Potato Fritters	50
Cauliflower	Sticky Cauliflower Wings	53

Lacto-Fermented Vegetables

This simple recipe uses the lactic acid bacteria naturally present on veggies, in the air, or even on your hands to preserve and enhance your vegetables' natural flavors. A single jar of fermented vegetables can contain hundreds of different strains of beneficial bacteria. The great thing is that lacto-fermentation not only gives you that typical tangy flavor but also lowers the pH of the food, creating an acidic environment that inhibits the growth of harmful bacteria. Lacto-fermentation can also improve the nutritional value of certain vegetables by enhancing the bioavailability of nutrients like vitamins B and C. It can even produce additional nutrients like vitamin K2, which is important for bones and health.

I haven't given any quantities here, because you can adapt this recipe depending on the quantity of vegetables you have available, and the number and size of jars you want to use.

Prep time 20 minutes

Fermentation time 7–14 days, depending on temperature and desired sourness

Ingredients

any raw vegetables, such as green beans, carrot sticks, broccoli or cauliflower florets, beets, onions, peppers, radishes, or cucumbers

seasonings, such as dill, black peppercorns, cumin seeds, bay leaves, and garlic cloves (optional)

salt

Equipment

sterilized jar(s)

- -

Prepare the vegetables Thoroughly wash your chosen vegetables, then cut them into uniform sizes, such as sticks or florets, to ensure even fermentation.

Prepare the brine Take a measuring cup and pour in enough water to fully submerge the vegetables in your chosen jar(s). Add 1tsp (5g) salt for every 6½ tbsp (100ml) water and stir to dissolve.

Pack the jars If you're using seasonings, place these at the bottom of the sterilized jar(s), then tightly pack the prepared vegetables into the jar(s), leaving about 1in (2.5cm) of space at the top. Pour the brine over the vegetables, ensuring that they are all fully submerged. You may need to use a fermentation weight or a small clean object to keep the vegetables below the brine.

Seal Cover the jar(s) with the lid(s), but not too tightly, as gases produced during fermentation need to escape. Alternatively, cover each jar with a cloth secured with a rubber band to allow airflow while keeping out contaminants.

Ferment Place the jar(s) in a cool, dark place (ideally 64–72°F/18–22°C). Allow to ferment for 7–14 days, depending on the temperature and your taste preference. Check daily to ensure the vegetables remain submerged. If mold forms on the surface, simply remove it and ensure the vegetables are submerged. Taste after a week, and continue fermenting until you reach your desired level of sourness.

Storage The vegetables are now ready to eat. To store, tighten the lid and transfer the jar(s) to the refrigerator. They will keep in the refrigerator for up to 6 months and will continue to develop flavor over time.

Vegetable Skin Powders

Ever wondered what to do with all those vegetable peels accumulating in your kitchen? Instead of throwing them out, you can turn them into a nutrient-rich powder! This zero-waste solution enhances the flavor and nutritional content of your meals while reducing food waste, making it ideal for sprinkling over your favorite foods. Use this creative and simple method to maximize the nutritional value of every part of your veggies and embrace sustainability. It doesn't have to be extremely intricate—I often find the most delicious things are the most straightforward. If you make this powder using beet peel, it can be used as a food coloring as well as a flavoring.

Prep time 10 minutes
Cooking time 5–60 minutes
(depending on the vegetables)

Ingredients

peel/skin from onions, garlic, beets, or carrots
optional flavorings (such as Mediterranean herbs, masala spice mix, chives, or dill)
salt and freshly ground black pepper

Prepare the peel Wash the vegetable peels or skins and pat them dry with a clean kitchen towel.

Preheat the oven Preheat the oven to 325°F (160°C).

Bake and dry Place the washed and dried peels on a baking sheet in a single layer. Bake them in the preheated oven until nice and crispy: about 5 minutes for garlic or onion skins, 20 minutes for carrot peels, and 30–60 minutes for beet peels (check them regularly). Once this is done, turn off the oven and leave the door shut to let the peels dry completely.

Blend Once the skins or peels are completely dry, transfer them to a blender or food processor. Blend until you have a fine powder consistency.

Season Season with salt and pepper, along with any optional flavorings. The amount you'll need will depend on the amount of powder you have and your taste preferences. Taste and adjust accordingly to achieve the desired flavor.

Storage Transfer the vegetable peel powder to an airtight container. Store it in a cool, dry place, away from direct sunlight. It will last for several months.

Prepare the peel

Bake and dry

Blend

Store

Upside-Down Onion Tart

What's not to love about golden caramelized onions wrapped in flaky puff pastry? With just a few simple ingredients, you can turn a few humble onions into a show-stopping meal that will impress all your guests, and it takes just a few minutes to make. You can adapt this recipe using almost any vegetable, but I find onions to be the perfect choice as they bring an incredible flavor.

Serves 4–6

Prep time 20 minutes

Cooking time 40–45 minutes

Ingredients

4 tbsp plant-based butter

3–4 onions, each sliced into 6–8 even-sized wedges from root to tip

2 tbsp water

3 tbsp maple syrup

2 tbsp balsamic vinegar

⅛ tsp salt

freshly ground black pepper

1 x 10½oz (320g) sheet plant-based ready-rolled puff pastry

3½oz (100g) plant-based cheddar cheese, grated

1 tsp picked fresh thyme leaves

Preheat the oven Preheat the oven to 425°F (220°C).

Caramelize the onions Melt the plant-based butter in an ovenproof skillet or cast-iron pan over medium heat. Add the onion wedges and sauté for 10–15 minutes, turning occasionally, until the onions are soft and starting to caramelize evenly. Add the water, along with the maple syrup, balsamic vinegar, and salt. Season to taste with black pepper. Cook for 5 minutes more until the mixture thickens and the onions are well coated.

Assemble the tart Remove the pan from the heat and arrange the onion wedges in an even layer across the bottom of the pan. Unroll the puff pastry sheet and trim it to the size of your pan. Carefully lay the pastry sheet over the onions, tucking it in at the edges.

Bake Bake for 20–25 minutes, or until the puff pastry is golden brown and crispy.

Remove from the pan Remove the pan from the oven and let it cool for 5 minutes, then run a knife around the edge of the pan to loosen the tart. Place a large serving plate over the pan, then carefully invert the tart on to the plate, so the caramelized onions are on top.

Finish and serve Top the tart with the grated plant-based cheddar cheese and fresh thyme, then slice and serve warm.

Storage Store leftovers in an airtight container in the refrigerator for up to 3 days. Reheat in the oven at 400°F (200°C) until warmed through and crispy.

Confit Garlic with Garden Herbs

We love eating garlic as much as we love growing it. Every year in around October or November, we plant as many garlic cloves as we can so we can have a stock for the following season. There are many ways to prepare and use garlic, but one of the things that we make most is confit garlic. It is quick, easy, and so delicious that the very thought of it makes me run to the kitchen to make some!

Makes 1 × 9fl oz (250ml) jar

Prep time 10 minutes

Cooking time 1 hour

Ingredients

1 cup plus 1 tablespoon (250ml) olive oil

small handful of thyme sprigs

small handful of rosemary sprigs

½ tsp chili flakes (optional, for an extra kick)

1–2 garlic bulbs, cloves separated and peeled

salt and freshly ground black pepper

- -

Infuse the olive oil with herbs Heat the olive oil in a saucepan over low heat. Add the thyme, rosemary, and chili flakes, if using, and leave for about 5 minutes to infuse the oil with their flavors.

Add the garlic Once the oil is infused, add the garlic cloves to the saucepan. Make sure they are fully submerged in the oil. Simmer the garlic in the infused olive oil for about 1 hour. The garlic should become tender and creamy but not browned. Keep an eye on the heat to ensure the garlic cooks gently without frying.

Season Season the confit garlic with salt and pepper to taste.

Cool Once cooked, remove the saucepan from the heat and let the confit garlic cool in the oil.

Storage Once cooled, transfer the garlic cloves and infused oil to a clean airtight container. Store in the refrigerator for up to 2 weeks.

Crispy Potato and Carrot Skin Snacks

Don't throw away those skins! How many times growing up did we see our parents and grandparents peeling potatoes and carrots, only to discard the skins? Thousands! Well, our generation's trend is skin-on fries, so let's embrace that instead. And if you do need to peel your veggies, make sure you use those peels to make the most delicious snacks!

Serves 2–3
Prep time 5 minutes
Cooking time 15 minutes

Ingredients
peelings of 10 carrots
peelings of 10 potatoes
½ tsp paprika
2 garlic cloves, minced (optional)
1 tbsp olive oil
salt and freshly ground black pepper

- - - - - - - - - - - - - - - - - -

Preheat the oven Preheat the oven to 350°F (180°C) and line a baking sheet with parchment paper.

Season Make sure the vegetable peelings are clean and dry. Pour them into a mixing bowl, and add the paprika and minced garlic, if using. Season with a pinch of salt and pepper and drizzle with olive oil. Toss the skins with the seasoning mixture until they are evenly coated.

Bake Spread the skins in a single layer on the prepared baking sheet. Bake for about 15 minutes, turning them every 5 minutes to ensure they cook evenly and don't burn, until golden brown and crispy.

Cool and serve Remove from the oven and cool slightly before serving.

Storage Store any leftover crispy skins in an airtight container at room temperature for up to 2 days. Reheat in the oven for a few minutes to restore crispiness, if desired.

Fresh Carrot Juice

Carrot juice is our go-to for a refreshing, health-boosting drink. Its vibrant orange color and natural sweetness make it both delicious and invigorating. It is also a great alternative for people who don't like to eat carrots raw but still want to introduce the many beneficial aspects of this root vegetable into their diet. Save any pulp to make our Carrot Cupcakes on page 43.

Serves 4
Prep time 5 minutes

Ingredients
2¼lb (1kg) carrots, washed, trimmed and roughly chopped

- - - - - - - - - - - - - - - - - -

Juice Simply add the carrots to your juicer and juice.

Serve Pour into glasses and enjoy immediately.

Carrot-Top Pesto

Fresh Carrot Juice

Crispy Potato and Carrot Skin Snacks

Carrot-Top Pesto

Did you know those leafy tops on your carrots are not only edible but also delicious? Next time you're at the farmers' market, make sure to tell your vendor to leave the greens on. Those deep green fronds are incredibly versatile, plus they're already included in the price of your carrots! Our favorite way to enjoy these delicious greens? Transforming them into a rich, herbaceous carrot-top pesto, which can be used as a sauce for pasta, a spread for sandwiches, or a dip for vegetables.

Makes about 1 cup (240ml)
Prep time 10 minutes

Ingredients

2-4 bunches green carrot tops
½ cup (65g) pine nuts
5 tbsp plus 1 tsp (80ml) olive oil
1 garlic clove
1 tsp lemon juice (optional, to preserve color)
salt and freshly ground black pepper

- -

Prepare the carrot tops Wash and thoroughly dry the carrot tops. Remove any tough stems.

Blend In a food processor, combine the carrot tops, pine nuts, olive oil, garlic, and lemon juice (if using). Season with salt and pepper, and pulse until a smooth paste forms, scraping down the sides as needed. Adjust the seasoning to taste.

Storage Use immediately, or transfer to an airtight container and store in the refrigerator for up to 1 week.

Carrot Turkish Truffles

When you juice or blend carrots, save the pulp, freeze it, and turn it into these delightful truffles whenever you're craving something special.

Makes 15–20 truffles
Prep time 20 minutes
Cooking time 10 minutes

Ingredients

pulp from 9–10 juiced carrots
1 cup (200g) caster sugar
2 tbsp water
1½ cups (150g) shredded coconut or almond flour
2 tbsp lemon juice
ground pistachios, for rolling

Prepare the carrot mixture In a medium saucepan, combine the carrot pulp, sugar, and water. Cook over medium heat, stirring constantly, until the sugar dissolves and the mixture thickens slightly—this should take 5-7 minutes. Remove the saucepan from the heat and stir in the shredded coconut or almond flour and lemon juice, mixing until well combined. The mixture should now be thick enough to shape into balls. If it's too wet, add a bit more coconut or almond flour.

Shape the truffles Once the mixture is cool enough to handle, take small portions (about a tablespoon each) and roll them into small balls using your hands.

Roll in pistachios Add the ground pistachios to a shallow bowl and roll each truffle in the pistachios to coat evenly.

Serve Arrange the truffles on a serving plate. These can be served immediately or chilled in the refrigerator for a firmer texture.

Storage Store the truffles in an airtight container in the refrigerator for up to 5 days. You can also freeze the truffles for up to 2 months. Thaw in the refrigerator before serving.

Carrot Cupcakes

How many times have we cleaned the juicer, only to discard that leftover pulp? And how often have we baked carrot cupcakes, spending so much time shredding carrots? With this recipe, your low-waste approach makes life easier. The pulp from your morning juices (see p40) is already perfectly minced and ready to be transformed into mind-blowing cupcakes that will easily compete with the ones you buy from your local coffee shop. For the coconut cream, simply refrigerate a can of coconut milk and then scoop the solid top layer from the can.

Makes 12 cupcakes
Prep time 15 minutes
Cooking time 20 minutes

Ingredients

1½ cups (185g) all-purpose flour
1 tsp baking soda
1 tbsp baking powder
1 tsp ground ginger
½ tsp ground nutmeg
¾ cup (150g) coconut sugar
½ cup (40g) shredded coconut
14–18oz (400–500g) carrot pulp (from your juicer)
1 cup (250g) plant-based yogurt
4 tbsp coconut oil, melted
zest of 1 lemon
orange zest, to decorate

For the frosting

1½ cups (180g) cashews
½ cup (120ml) coconut cream (see recipe introduction)
2 tbsp maple syrup
pinch of salt
zest of 1 lemon
seeds of 1 vanilla pod

- -

Soak the cashews Soak the cashews for the frosting in a bowl of water overnight (or for 20 minutes in hot water if you don't have time).

Preheat the oven Preheat the oven to 400°F (200°C). Line a muffin pan with cupcake liners.

Mix In a bowl, mix together the flour, baking soda, baking powder, ginger, nutmeg, coconut sugar, and coconut. In a separate bowl, combine the carrot pulp, yogurt, melted coconut oil, and lemon zest. Pour the wet ingredients into the bowl of dry ingredients and gently fold together until just combined.

Bake Divide the batter evenly among the prepared cupcake liners, filling each about two-thirds full. Bake for about 20 minutes, or until a toothpick inserted into the center of a cupcake comes out clean.

Cool Remove the cupcakes from the oven and let cool completely on a wire rack before frosting.

Prepare the frosting Drain the soaked cashews and pour into a blender. Add the coconut cream, maple syrup, salt, lemon zest, and vanilla. Blend until smooth and creamy.

Frost the cupcakes Once the cupcakes are cooled, frost them generously with the prepared frosting. Grate some orange zest on top for extra flavor.

Storage Store the frosted cupcakes in an airtight container in the refrigerator for up to 4 days. Any leftover frosting can be stored in an airtight container in the fridge for up to a week.

Ginger Shot

Ginger is not actually a root but a rhizome—an underground stem that produces roots and new shoots. This immune system-boosting ginger shot is perfect for cold and flu season, and I've also shared a curry mix to use up the leftover pulp. Below you will find a ginger "bug"—a homemade soda bursting with probiotics—to complete the trio of gingery goodness.

Makes 3–4
Prep time 10 minutes

Ingredients
3 thumb-sized pieces of ginger

Optional extras
1 tsp ground turmeric
1 tsp freshly ground black pepper
1 orange
1 carrot

- - - - - - - - - - - - - - - - - - - -

Juice Add the ginger to your juicer, along with the other ingredients (if using), and juice.

Storage Serve right away, or store in the refrigerator for up to 1 week.

Curry Powder Mix

Makes 1 cup (140g)
Prep time 15 minutes

Ingredients
2 tbsp curry powder
3 tbsp ginger pulp (leftover from juicing)
2 tbsp ground black pepper
2 tbsp fennel seeds
2 tbsp fenugreek seeds

1 tbsp ground turmeric
1 tbsp mustard seeds
2 tbsp cayenne powder
1 tbsp coriander seeds (optional)
1 tbsp cumin seeds (optional)

Equipment
dehydrator

- - - - - - - - - - - - - - - - - - - -

Dehydrate the pulp Spread out the ginger pulp on a dehydrator tray and dehydrate overnight at 120°F (50°C) until it's completely dry.

Blend Add the dried pulp to a blender with the remaining spices. Blend to a fine powder consistency.

Storage Store in an airtight container for up to a year.

Ginger Bug

Makes 1 starter or bug
Prep time 5 minutes
Fermentation time 5–7 days

Ingredients
14 tbsp finely chopped or grated fresh ginger (skin on)
14 tbsp sugar (you can use any type, but I prefer to use organic)
2 cups (475ml) water

Day 1: Mix Add 2 tablespoons of the ginger and 2 tablespoons of the sugar to the jar, and pour in the water. Stir well to dissolve the sugar. Cover the jar with a cloth or a loose lid to allow air to circulate while keeping out any debris or insects.

Days 2–7: Feed Each day for the next week, add an additional 2 tablespoons chopped ginger and 2 tablespoons sugar to "feed" it. Stir the mixture once or twice a day. By about day 5, you should see small bubbles forming, indicating that fermentation is occurring. The mixture should also have a pleasant, slightly yeasty smell. Once the ginger bug is active (bubbling), it's ready to be used to ferment homemade soda (see opposite).

Storage Store the ginger bug in a jar with a lid in the refrigerator. To keep it alive, feed it weekly with 1 tablespoon ginger and 1 tablespoon sugar. If you plan to use it more frequently, keep it at room temperature and feed it daily.

Ginger
Bug

Curry
Powder

Ginger
Shot

Homemade ginger soda

» To make your own ginger soda, strain ½ cup (120ml) of your ginger bug (return the strained solids to the jar) and mix it with about 7 cups (1.7 liters) of your favorite fresh organic juice (make sure there are no chemicals, or they will kill off the beneficial bacteria provided by the ginger bug). Pour the mixture into sterilized glass bottles with flip tops, leaving ½in (1cm) space at the top. Let ferment for 2–3 days at room temperature. The carbonation process will start making your soda fizzy. Transfer the bottle to the refrigerator, where it will keep for up to 2 months (chilling it will slow down the carbonation and fermentation processes).

Stuffed Flatbread

This recipe is all about turning leftovers into a culinary masterpiece. Iasmina's grandmother used to bake this for her, and now this flatbread is my comfort food of choice. The combination of creamy mashed potatoes, rich plant-based cheese, and tangy sun-dried tomatoes wrapped in a soft, homemade flatbread is just unbeatable. It's the perfect example of how simple ingredients can create something extraordinary with a little creativity.

Makes 4–6

Prep time 15 minutes
Cooking time 15 minutes

Ingredients

1 cup (250g) plant-based yogurt
1¼ cups (175g) self-rising flour
pinch of salt

For the filling

2½ cups (675g) mashed potatoes
3½oz (100g) plant-based cheese, grated
2oz (60g) sun-dried tomatoes
2–3 tsp of your favorite freshly chopped herbs, such as parsley, sage, and cilantro, plus extra to serve
3 black garlic cloves (or 1 regular garlic clove), mashed

Prepare the dough In a large bowl, combine the flour, plant-based yogurt, and a pinch of salt, and mix to form a dough. Divide the dough into 4–6 small balls and roll out using a rolling pin until thin.

Prepare the filling In another large bowl, mix together the mashed potatoes, plant-based cheese, sun-dried tomatoes, herbs, and garlic.

Stuff and seal Place 2 tablespoons of the filling on top of each piece of dough, then gather the edges of the dough and close them around the filling, using a little water to seal.

Cook and serve Heat a nonstick skillet over medium heat. Working in batches, cook each flatbread for 2–3 minutes on each side until golden brown. Serve the stuffed flatbreads with a sprinkle of fresh herbs or your favorite dips.

Storage Any leftover stuffed flatbreads will keep in an airtight container in the refrigerator for up to 2 days.

Potato Noodles

We used to make gnocchi with my grandma every Sunday and invite the whole family to enjoy them for lunch. My role was to hide under the dining table and try to nick as many ingredients as possible before she caught me and kicked me out of the kitchen. This is a revised recipe combining my passion for Italian and Asian food. These are delicious with my Vegan Arrabbiata Sauce (see opposite).

Serves 2–4
Prep time 30 minutes
Cooking time 5–10 minutes

Ingredients

1½ cups (400g) leftover mashed potatoes (ensure they are not overly seasoned or creamy)
½ cup (65g) all-purpose flour, plus extra for dusting
¼ (35g) cup potato starch
½ tsp salt, plus extra for cooking
¼ tsp freshly ground black pepper (optional)
¼ tsp garlic powder or onion powder (optional)
olive oil, plant-based butter, or Vegan Arrabbiata Sauce (see opposite), to serve

- -

Mix the dough In a large mixing bowl, combine all the ingredients, and mix until they come together to form a dough. If the dough is too sticky, add a bit more flour. If it's too dry, add a small amount of water, a tablespoon at a time, until it comes together.

Form the noodles Lightly flour your work surface to prevent sticking. Divide the dough into manageable portions, and roll each portion into a long, thick, sausage-shaped log, about ½in (1cm) thick and 8in (20cm) long. Use extra flour if needed to prevent sticking.

Cook Bring a large pot of salted water to a boil. Carefully drop the noodles into the boiling water. Cook for 5–10 minutes, or until they float to the surface and are tender. Freshly made noodles cook quickly, so keep an eye on them. Use a slotted spoon to remove the noodles from the pot and drain well.

Serve Toss the cooked noodles with a bit of olive oil or plant-based butter, or with my Arrabbiata Sauce.

Storage Leftover cooked noodles can be stored in an airtight container in the refrigerator for up to 3 days. Reheat by briefly sautéing or microwaving.

Vegan Arrabbiata Sauce

Serves 4

Prep time 15 minutes

Cooking time 20 minutes

Ingredients

2 tbsp olive oil

4 garlic cloves, minced

½ tsp dried chili flakes, or to taste

1 x 14oz (400g) can chopped
   tomatoes

2 tbsp tomato purée

1 tsp dried oregano

1 tsp dried basil

½ tsp salt, or to taste

¼ tsp freshly ground black
   pepper, or to taste

1 tsp caster sugar (optional, to
   balance acidity)

chopped parsley or basil leaves,
   to serve (optional)

Sauté the garlic and tomatoes Heat the oil in a medium saucepan over medium heat. Add the garlic and chili flakes, and sauté for about 1 minute until fragrant, being careful not to burn the garlic. Add the tomatoes and tomato purée, and stir well to combine.

Add seasoning Stir in the oregano, basil, salt, and black pepper. Taste the sauce, and adjust the seasoning if needed. If desired, you can add the sugar to balance the acidity.

Simmer Bring the sauce to a simmer, then reduce the heat to low and let it cook for 15–20 minutes, stirring occasionally, until it thickens and the flavors meld together.

Serve Enjoy with cooked potato noodles (see opposite), garnish with fresh basil or parsley if you like.

Storage Leftover sauce can be stored in an airtight container in the refrigerator for up to 1 week. It can also be frozen for up to 3 months.

Potato Fritters

Who doesn't love a good fritter? These potato fritters are my homage to the Italian tradition of making the most out of simple ingredients. Infused with olive oil and a touch of sweetness, these fritters are crispy on the outside, and soft and flavorful on the inside. They're a real testament to the versatility of potatoes. Usually served during carnival period, these fritters are proven crowd-pleasers that are sure to delight.

Serves 4–6

Prep time 20 minutes, plus proofing time

Cooking time 15 minutes

Ingredients

2 tsp active dry yeast

2 tbsp superfine sugar

4 cups (950ml) water

2 cups (270g) all-purpose flour

⅔ cup (150g) mashed potatoes

2 tbsp olive oil

1 tsp baking powder

1 tsp salt

vegetable oil, for deep-frying

For dusting

powdered sugar

ground cinnamon

- -

Activate the yeast In a bowl, combine the yeast and sugar with the water. Stir and leave to sit for about 10 minutes until frothy.

Mix the batter In a separate large bowl, mix together the flour, mashed potatoes, olive oil, baking powder, and salt. Once activated, pour in the frothy yeast mixture and mix to form a smooth batter.

Proof Cover with a clean kitchen towel and proof at room temperature for 1–2 hours until the mixture doubles in size.

Fry Pour oil into a deep-sided frying pan to a depth of 2in (5cm) and place over medium-high heat. You can tell the oil is hot enough for frying by dropping a small amount of batter into the pan; if it sizzles and floats, you're ready to go. Working in batches, drop spoonfuls of the batter into the hot oil and fry for 1–2 minutes until golden brown on both sides. Remove from the oil with a slotted spoon and set aside on a plate lined with paper towels while you fry the rest.

Dust and serve Dust the potato fritters with powdered sugar and cinnamon before serving warm.

Storage These potato fritters are best enjoyed fresh but will keep for 1 day stored in an airtight container at room temperature.

Sticky Cauliflower Wings

Imagine the most delicious bite-sized wings, coated in a flavorful batter, baked or pan-fried to crisp perfection, and then tossed in a sticky, sweet, and sometimes spicy sauce. And the best part? No chicken involved—these are cauliflower wings.

Serves 2–4, depending on the size of the cauliflower

Prep time 30 minutes

Cooking time 20–30 minutes

Ingredients

1 cauliflower

¾ cup (90g) all-purpose flour

½ cup (120ml) plant-based milk

¼ tsp garlic powder

½ tsp salt

¼ tsp freshly ground black pepper

panko bread crumbs, to coat

green onions, sliced, to garnish

For the sticky sauce

4 tbsp dark soy sauce

⅔ cup (160ml) maple syrup

1 tsp cornstarch

1 tsp sesame seeds, plus extra to serve

pinch of ground ginger

Preheat the oven Preheat the oven to 350°F (200°C).

Prepare the wings Separate the leaves from the cauliflower and save to use in another recipe. Separate out the cauliflower florets, breaking them off into "wing"-like shapes.

Mix the batter In a large bowl, mix together the flour, milk, garlic powder, salt, and black pepper and stir to form a smooth batter.

Coat and bake Pour the panko bread crumbs into a shallow bowl. Dip the cauliflower pieces into the batter, then toss in the bread crumbs to coat. Transfer to a baking sheet and bake for 20–30 minutes, depending on desired crunchiness.

Prepare the sticky sauce Meanwhile, make the sauce. In a saucepan over low heat, combine the soy sauce, maple syrup, cornstarch, sesame seeds, and ginger with ½ cup (120ml) water. Stir and cook for about 10 minutes until thickened.

Coat the wings When the baked cauliflower wings are ready, pour over the sauce and toss to coat evenly.

Garnish and serve Garnish with green onions and sesame seeds and serve.

Storage Best served fresh but can be stored in the refrigerator for 1-2 days. Reheat before serving.

Grains and Pulses

Amaranth	Popped Amaranth Chocolate Bark	56
	Amaranth Leaf Dal	59
Oats	Oat Milk	60
	Oat Pulp Granola	61
Rice	Arancini	62
	Rice Bread	64
Beans	Feijoada	66
Chickpeas	Rainbow Falafel	68
	Chickpea Chocolate Mousse	71
Lentils	Red Lentil Crêpes	72

Popped Amaranth Chocolate Bark

We like growing amaranth for its unique look and flavor. Around September, we cut the plants at the base and hang them upside down in the greenhouse to dry. You can turn amaranth into a quick, grab-and-go treat that hits the spot when you need a boost of energy. Toss it into your favorite dried fruits or nuts for extra crunch, or make this delicious chocolate bark.

Makes 8–12 pieces

Prep time 10 minutes

Cooking time 10 minutes

Ingredients

1 cup (15g) amaranth

7oz (200g) dark chocolate, broken into pieces

1 tsp coconut oil

1 tsp peanut butter (optional)

Pop the amaranth Place a large, dry skillet over medium-high heat. It's important that the pan is hot but not smoking. Once the pan is hot, add a small amount of amaranth (about 1–2 tablespoons). Make sure you don't overcrowd the pan; it's best to pop the amaranth in batches.

Cover the pan with a lid to prevent the amaranth from jumping out as it pops. Shake the pan gently and listen out for the popping sound—it should be similar to that made by popcorn, but quieter and less frequent.

After 1–2 minutes, or once the popping slows down, remove the pan from heat. Transfer the popped amaranth to a bowl to cool. Repeat the process until all the amaranth is popped.

Melt the chocolate Melt the dark chocolate pieces and coconut oil in a heatproof bowl set over a pan of simmering water, stirring until fully melted and combined. Alternatively, you can melt them in a microwave in 30-second bursts, stirring in between each one, until the chocolate is smooth and fully melted. If using peanut butter, stir it into the melted chocolate until well combined.

Mix In a large bowl, combine the popped amaranth with the melted chocolate mixture, stirring until evenly coated. If you like, you can reserve a few pieces of popped amaranth for decoration.

Spread and set Line a baking sheet with parchment paper. Pour the chocolate and amaranth mixture on to the parchment paper and spread it out evenly with a spatula. If you reserved any pieces of popped amaranth, sprinkle them on top for a decorative touch. Place the baking sheet in the refrigerator or freezer to set. This will take 20–30 minutes.

Break and serve Once set, break the chocolate bark into pieces and enjoy.

Storage Store in an airtight container at room temperature for up to 1 week, or in the refrigerator for up to 2 weeks. You can also freeze for up to 3 months. Thaw at room temperature before serving.

Amaranth

» Amaranth is a showstopper in any garden. It comes in different colors, ranging from golden brown and deep red to bright green. You need to be careful about the area in which you choose to grow it, as it seeds freely and the next year you will have amaranth plants popping up everywhere. It is incredibly versatile in the kitchen, and we always have a jar of it in our pantry. Better yet, the seeds are not the only edible part—the leaves can also be used for a meal packed with an array of great flavors (see p58).

Amaranth Leaf Dal

Amaranth leaves, with their earthy flavor, can be used just like spinach, and we love cooking them into a delicious dal. Imagine a pot of hearty, organic dal simmering away, packed with the fresh goodness of amaranth leaves. It is guaranteed to take a cozy night at home to the next level and is perfect for a cold day when you just want to stay home by yourself or with your loved ones. We like to serve this with rice, flatbreads, or roti.

Serves 4

Prep time 10 minutes

Cooking time 20 minutes

Ingredients

1–2 handfuls of amaranth leaves, washed and chopped

1 cup (175g) split red lentils

½ tsp ground turmeric

3 tbsp vegetable oil

1 tsp cumin seeds

4–6 garlic cloves, finely chopped

1 onion, chopped

1 large tomato, chopped

1 tsp ground cumin

salt

To serve

handful of cilantro, chopped

chili flakes

Cook the dal Place the amaranth leaves, lentils, and turmeric in a large saucepan. Pour in enough water to cover the lentils by about ¾in (2cm). Bring to a boil, then simmer for about 10 minutes until the lentils are tender.

Prepare the spice mixture Heat the vegetable oil in a separate saucepan over medium heat. Add the cumin seeds, garlic, and onion, and sauté for 5 minutes until golden brown. Add the tomato and ground cumin, season with salt and cook for a little longer until pulpy.

Combine Add the spice mixture to the cooked dal and simmer for a couple of minutes until combined. Add more water if you prefer a runnier texture.

Serve Sprinkle over the cilantro and chili flakes to serve, and enjoy hot with your chosen accompaniments.

Storage Store any leftover dal in an airtight container in the refrigerator for 3–4 days. Reheat gently before serving.

Oat Milk

Oats were something we discovered when we moved to London, as they're not so typical in Italy. As we transitioned to a plant-based diet, we experimented with oats in countless ways, from making our own oat milk to baking cookies and creating energy bites. This versatile ingredient quickly became a favorite and a must-have item that's always fully stocked in our pantry.

Stop buying store-bought plant-based milk and start making your own at home! It's the easiest, most natural way to enjoy a healthier drink, free from artificial additives. Plus, you save money, you get to customize the flavor to your liking, and it takes literally five minutes from start to finish.

Makes 1 quart (1 liter)
Prep time 5 minutes

Ingredients
1 cup (90g) old-fashioned oats
2 dates, pitted
½ teaspoon salt
seeds from 1 vanilla pod

- -

Blend In a blender, combine the oats, dates, salt, and vanilla with 4¼ cups (1 liter) water. Blend until smooth.

Strain Pour the blended mixture through a nut-milk bag, muslin, or fine mesh sieve to strain out any solids. Squeeze or press to extract as much liquid as possible.

Storage Transfer the oat milk to a clean container with a lid. Store in the refrigerator for up to 5 days. Shake well before using.

Oat Pulp Granola

Instead of buying granola from the store, make your own using the leftover pulp of your homemade oat milk (see opposite). It is extremely simple, and you can make a big batch to store in a jar and enjoy every morning with yogurt or instead of cereal. It is crunchy and sweet and requires minimal effort and energy to make.

Serves 4-6

Prep time 10 minutes

Cooking time 30-35 minutes

Ingredients

4 tbsp coconut oil

4 tbsp maple syrup

2 cups (250-300g) oat pulp (left over from making oat milk, see opposite)

¼ cup (60g) mixed nuts, roughly chopped (such as almonds, walnuts, or cashews)

½ cup (15g) puffed quinoa

1 tbsp sunflower seeds

Preheat the oven Preheat the oven to 375°F (190°C) and line a baking sheet with parchment paper for easy cleanup.

Combine the coconut oil and maple syrup Melt the coconut oil in a small saucepan over low heat. Stir in the maple syrup until well combined. Remove from the heat and set aside.

Mix the granola In a large mixing bowl, combine the oat pulp, chopped mixed nuts, puffed quinoa, and sunflower seeds. Pour the melted coconut oil and maple syrup mixture over the dry ingredients, and stir until everything is evenly coated.

Bake Pour the mixture on to the prepared baking sheet and spread it out evenly. Bake for 20-25 minutes, stirring halfway through, until the granola is golden brown and crispy. Keep an eye on it to prevent it from burning.

Cool Let the granola cool completely on the baking sheet. It will become crispier as it cools. Once completely cool, you can serve or store.

Serve Enjoy the granola with your favorite plant-based yogurt or milk, or use it as a topping for smoothies, oatmeal, or even salads.

Storage Store in an airtight container at room temperature for up to 2 weeks. For longer storage, you can refrigerate the granola for up to 1 month. You can also freeze the granola for up to 3 months. Thaw at room temperature before serving.

Arancini

This is our go-to vegan arancini recipe. I love making it for my Sicilian dad.

Makes 8–10 arancini
Prep time 30 minutes
Cooking time 50 minutes

Ingredients

vegetable oil, for deep-frying
bread crumbs, for coating

For the rice (or use 3 cups/500g leftover risotto)

1 tbsp olive oil
1 onion, finely chopped
2 garlic cloves, finely chopped
1 celery stick, finely chopped
3 cups (500g) leftover cooked rice
6½ tbsp (100ml) vegetable stock
salt and freshly ground black pepper

For the filling

3 tbsp olive oil
3 garlic cloves, minced
1 onion, finely chopped
1 celery stick, finely chopped
1 small carrot, finely chopped
4½oz (125g) plant-based ground "meat"
3 tbsp vegetable stock
9oz (250g) tomato purée, plus extra to serve
1 cup (200g) peas (optional)
9oz (250g) plant-based cheese, grated (optional)

Prepare the rice mixture If you are using leftover risotto, skip this step. Heat the olive oil in a skillet over medium heat. Add the onion, garlic, and celery, and fry for 3–5 minutes until starting to turn golden, stirring all the while, then add the rice and stock. Season to taste with salt and pepper. Cook for 10–15 minutes until the mixture is sticky but not too oily. Set aside to cool.

Prepare the filling Heat the olive oil in a saucepan over low heat and make a sofrito by slowly cooking the garlic, onion, celery, and carrot for 3–5 minutes until golden. Add the plant-based ground "meat," followed by the stock and tomato purée. Season with salt and pepper and add the peas, if using. Simmer for 20–30 minutes.

Shape Once the rice mixture has cooled, you can shape the arancini. Take enough mixture to form a ball about 2in (5cm) in diameter. Press the middle with your thumb to make it into a bowl shape, then add 1 teaspoon of the filling to the middle. If you like, you can add a little plant-based cheese, too, ensuring a gooey, melted center when cooked. Bring the edges up to cover the filling and form into a ball once more.

Coat and fry Pour oil into a deep saucepan to a depth of 6in (15cm) and place over medium-high heat. While the oil is heating, roll the shaped arancini in the bread crumbs to coat. To check if the oil is ready, dip the handle of a wooden spoon or chopstick into the pan. If the oil starts steadily bubbling around the stick, it's hot enough. If the bubbles are vigorous, the oil might be too hot, and if only a few or no bubbles form, it's not hot enough. Once the oil is ready, carefully add the arancini, working in batches of 2 or 3 at a time to avoid overcrowding the pan, and fry for 1–2 minutes until golden brown. Remove from the oil with a slotted spoon and set aside on a plate lined with paper towels while you make the rest.

Serve Plate up the arancini while hot, with a side of tomato purée for dipping.

Storage Refrigerate in an airtight container for up to 3 days. Best served fresh.

～～～～～～

Using leftover rice

» You should cool freshly cooked rice as soon as possible, within the first hour, and refrigerate immediately. When reheating, make sure the rice is steaming hot all the way through. It should reach a temperature of at least 165°F (74°C).

Add filling

Shape

Close into a ball

Coat and fry

Rice Bread

Can you believe that rice is one of the most wasted foods in the world? But there are countless ways to breathe new life into this versatile grain and enjoy its flavors in unexpected ways. Using just a small amount of rice, you can create this delightful, spongy and gluten-free loaf. It's not only cost-effective but also a great way to use rice as a flour alternative. It has all the fluffiness of normal bread.

Serves 6–8

Prep time 15 minutes, plus soaking and proofing time

Cooking time 40 minutes

Ingredients

1¾ cups (360g) raw white rice
  (any kind will work)
4 tbsp vegetable oil
1 tsp salt
2 tbsp (25g) superfine sugar
2¼ tsp (8g) fast-acting dry yeast

- -

Soak the rice Pour the rice into a bowl and add over enough water to cover. Let soak for 4–5 hours.

Blend Strain the soaked rice and transfer it to a blender. Add the remaining ingredients to the blender, along with 1 cup (240ml) fresh water. Blend until a smooth batter forms.

Proof Preheat the oven to 104–120°F (40–50°C). Pour the batter into a 2lb (900g) loaf pan and proof in the oven for 20 minutes.

Bake Remove the bread from the oven and increase the oven temperature to 375°F (190°C). Spray the bread with water to prevent the crust from burning. Once the oven is hot enough, return the bread to the oven and bake for 40 minutes until golden brown and cooked through. Let cool completely in the pan.

Storage Store in an airtight container at room temperature for 2–3 days. To keep the bread fresh for longer, refrigerate for up to a week. Best eaten when freshly baked.

Feijoada

Beans feijoada is a popular Brazilian favorite that adds warmth and comfort to any table. Growing up, Sundays were synonymous with the delectable aroma of feijoada cooking in the kitchen at my grandmother's house. Here, I've given this recipe a plant-based twist. Each bite of this rich stew, packed with varied beans and fragrant spices, evokes memories of family reunions and culinary traditions. The nicest part about this dish is that it is considered a "poor man's food," made from leftover scraps and low-cost ingredients. It is definitely one of my top-five favorites!

Serves 8
Prep time 10 minutes
Cooking time 1 hour 30 minutes

Ingredients
1 tbsp olive oil
1 onion, finely chopped
4 garlic cloves, minced
4 plant-based sausages, sliced (optional)
1lb (450g) dried black beans, soaked overnight, or 4 × 14oz (400g) cans black beans, drained and rinsed
3 cups (750ml) vegetable stock or water
2 bay leaves
2 tsp nutritional yeast
¼ tsp cayenne pepper
4 tbsp finely chopped flat-leaf parsley
salt

To serve
cooked white rice
diced tomatoes

- -

Fry the onion and garlic Heat the olive oil in a large pot or deep skillet over medium heat. Add the onion and garlic, and sauté for 5–7 minutes, or until the onion is softened and translucent.

Add the sausage (optional) If using, add the plant-based sausages to the pan and cook, stirring, for 4–5 minutes until browned and slightly crispy.

Make the stew If using soaked dried beans, drain them, and add them to the pot. If using canned beans, simply add them directly. Stir to combine, then pour in the vegetable stock or water—there should be enough to just cover the beans. Add the bay leaves, nutritional yeast, and cayenne pepper, and season with a pinch of salt. Stir well. Bring the mixture to a boil, then reduce the heat to low. Cover and let simmer gently for about 1 hour for dried beans or 30 minutes for canned beans, stirring occasionally to prevent sticking.

Finish Once the beans are tender and the stew has thickened, stir in the chopped parsley. Adjust the seasoning with more salt if needed. If the stew is too thick, you can add a bit more water or stock to reach your desired consistency.

Enjoy Serve the feijoada hot, ideally with white rice and diced tomatoes on the side.

Storage Store any leftovers in an airtight container in the refrigerator for 3–4 days. Reheat gently on the stove before serving.

Rainbow Falafel

Welcome to the vibrant world of rainbow falafel, where each bite is a burst of color and flavor. This twist on the classic Middle Eastern dish is not just visually stunning but also packed with nutrients. Integrating vegetables like beets, spinach, and butternut squash not only adds a spectrum of colors but also enhances the flavor profile.

Makes about 40 falafel (8 of each color)

Prep time 1 hour, plus overnight soaking

Cooking time 10 minutes

Ingredients

5 cups (1.1kg) dried chickpeas

5–10 garlic cloves, depending on how garlicky you like your falafel, finely chopped

1 large onion, finely chopped

3½oz (100g) mixed herbs, such as parsley, chives, and sage

juice of 1 lemon

5 tsp baking soda

potato starch, for dusting (optional)

vegetable oil, for deep-frying

salt and freshly ground black pepper

For the red falafel

3½oz (100g) beets

For the orange falafel

3½oz (100g) butternut squash, peeled

1 tsp ground turmeric

For the purple falafel

3½oz (100g) purple potato, peeled

For the green falafel

handful of spinach

handful of flat-leaf parsley

Soak the chickpeas Add the chickpeas into a large bowl and pour over enough water to cover. Let soak overnight.

Prepare the vegetables Preheat the oven to 375°F (190°C). Arrange the beets, butternut squash, and purple potato on a baking sheet, spaced well apart, and bake for 30–40 minutes until soft.

Make the falafel mixture Drain the soaked chickpeas, then pour into a large bowl. Add the garlic cloves, onion, herbs, and lemon juice, and season with salt and pepper.

Add the colors Divide the chickpea mixture equally among 5 bowls. Add the beets to the first bowl, the steamed squash and turmeric to the second, the purple potato to the third, and the spinach and parsley to the fourth. Leave the fifth plain.

Blend One at a time, add the contents of each bowl into a blender and blend to combine, then remove and move on to the next bowl. You will end up with 5 different-colored falafel mixes.

Add the baking soda Stir 1 teaspoon of baking soda into each bowl.

Form Using your hands, form each color of mixture into about 8 bite-sized balls. If the mix is too wet, roll the balls in a bit of potato starch to prevent them from sticking or falling apart during frying.

Fry Pour oil into a deep-sided skillet to a depth of 4in (10cm) and place over medium heat. The oil is hot enough for frying when a small amount of batter dropped into the pan sizzles and floats. Working in batches, add the falafels to the oil and fry for 1–2 minutes until they float and turn golden. Remove from the oil with a slotted spoon and set aside on a plate lined with paper towels while you fry the rest.

Serve Ear with your favorite dip, zingy pickles, and a fresh salad.

Storage Store in an airtight container in the fridge for up to 5 days. You can freeze any extra falafel before frying, then defrost and deep-fry them as needed.

Chickpea Chocolate Mousse

Surprising but true, canned chickpeas can offer the secret ingredient for a decadent chocolate mousse! Although I always enjoyed store-bought chocolate mousse as a child, as my cooking abilities improved, I made an effort to incorporate more nutritional content into everything I ate on a daily basis. If your kids have a craving for something sweet but still nutritious, this is the recipe for them. The mousse is light and airy, with a rich chocolate flavor that pairs perfectly with the crunchy pistachios and tart raspberries.

Serves 4–6
Prep time 30 minutes, plus chilling time

Ingredients
7oz (200g) high-quality dark chocolate (at least 70 percent cocoa), broken into pieces
½ cup (120ml) aquafaba (the liquid from canned chickpeas)
½ cup (100g) superfine sugar
1 tsp vanilla extract

To serve
plant-based whipped cream
roughly chopped pistachios
raspberries

- -

Melt the chocolate Melt the chocolate in a heatproof bowl set over a pan of simmering water. Stir occasionally until smooth and fully melted. Remove from the heat and let it cool slightly.

Whip the aquafaba In a large, clean mixing bowl, use an electric mixer to whip the aquafaba until stiff peaks form. This should take 5–10 minutes. Ensure your mixing bowl and beaters are free from any grease or oil, as this can prevent the aquafaba from whipping properly.

Mix Gradually add the sugar to the whipped aquafaba, continuing to whip between each addition until the sugar is fully dissolved and the mixture is glossy. Add the vanilla extract, then very gently fold the slightly cooled melted chocolate into the whipped aquafaba mixture. Be careful not to deflate the mixture; fold until fully combined and smooth.

Chill Spoon the mousse into individual serving glasses or bowls, then refrigerate for at least 2 hours, or until set.

Serve To serve, top each mousse with a dollop of whipped cream, a sprinkle of chopped pistachios, and a few fresh raspberries, then enjoy.

Storage Store leftover mousse in an airtight container in the refrigerator for up to 3 days. While not ideal for texture, the mousse can be frozen for up to 1 month. Thaw in the refrigerator before serving.

Red Lentil Crêpes

Switch up your breakfast game with these red lentil crêpes—they're thin, protein-packed, and incredibly versatile. Inspired by the traditional dosa, these crêpes are our go-to for a nutritious start to the day. Here I've given you two options: a savory version with garlic and herbs, or a sweet one topped with berries.

Makes 4–6 crêpes

Prep time 10 minutes, plus overnight soaking

Cooking time 15 minutes

Ingredients

1 cup (250g) split red lentils

½ tsp salt

2½ cups (600ml) water

For savory crêpes

1 tbsp (50g) fresh herbs of your choice (such as cilantro), finely chopped

2 garlic cloves, minced

freshly ground black pepper

For sweet crêpes

your favorite fruits

plant-based yogurt

plant-based caramel sauce or maple syrup

Soak the lentils Rinse the lentils in a colander, then pour into a bowl and add over enough water to cover. Let soak overnight.

Make the batter The next day, drain the lentils and pour into a blender, along with the salt and water. If you're making savory crêpes, add the herbs and garlic, and season to taste with black pepper. Blend to form a smooth batter, adding a little more water if needed.

Cook the crêpes Heat a nonstick skillet over medium heat. Pour a ladleful of batter into the center of the heated pan, and use the back of the ladle or a spatula to spread the batter in a circular motion to create a thin dosa-style crêpe. Cook for 1–2 minutes until the edges start to lift and the bottom is golden brown, then carefully flip and cook on the other side for 1 minute until golden brown. Transfer to a plate to keep warm, and repeat the process with the remaining batter, adjusting the heat as needed.

Serve Serve the red lentil crêpes warm. If you're making the savory version, try topping with a dollop of your favorite chutney. If you're making the sweet version, scatter over some fruit, then drizzle with yogurt and caramel sauce or maple syrup and enjoy.

Storage Store any leftover crêpes in an airtight container in the refrigerator for up to 2 days. Reheat before serving.

Nuts
and
Seeds

Hazelnuts	Hazelnut Milk	**76**
	Hazelnut Pulp and Chocolate Baklava	**76**
Almonds	Almond Pulp Amaretti Cookies	**79**
	Almond Milk	**80**
Coffee Beans	Tiramisu	**81**
Pistachios	Pistachio Milk	**82**
	Pistachio Blondies	**82**
Sesame Seeds	Black Sesame Seed Butter (Tahini)	**84**
Mustard Seeds	Homemade Mustard	**86**
Sunflower Seeds	Sunflower Butter	**87**

Hazelnut Milk

Hazelnut milk is one of our favorite dairy-free alternatives; it's creamy and rich and has a lot of body.

Makes 3 cups (750ml)
Prep time 10 minutes, plus overnight soaking

Ingredients
¾ cup (100g) hazelnuts
1 tbsp date paste
3 cups (750ml) water

- - - - - - - - - - - - - - - - - -

Soak Place the hazelnuts in a large bowl and pour over enough water to cover them by about 1in (2.5cm). Let soak for about 12 hours, or overnight.

Blend Drain and rinse the hazelnuts, then pour into a blender. Add the date paste and water, and blend on high until smooth. This should take around 2 minutes.

Strain Line a large bowl with a nut-milk bag or piece of muslin. Pour the hazelnut mixture into the bag or cloth, then squeeze well to extract as much milk as possible. Reserve the pulp for use in another recipe.

Storage Pour the strained hazelnut milk into a bottle. It will keep in the refrigerator for up to 5 days. It may separate, so give it a good shake before use.

Hazelnut Pulp and Chocolate Baklava

When thinking of ways to repurpose leftovers, our aim is to craft something decadent and delicious yet simple to make.

Makes 20–24 pieces
Prep time 30 minutes
Cooking time 20–25 minutes

Ingredients
3½–5oz (100–150g) hazelnut pulp (left over from making hazelnut milk; see left)
¼ cup (30g) crushed hazelnuts
1 tbsp cacao powder
2¼oz (70g) dark chocolate, chopped
4–5 tbsp plant-based butter
24 sheets store-bought phyllo pastry

For the syrup
1 cup (240ml) maple syrup

- -

Prepare the filling In a bowl, combine the hazelnut pulp, crushed hazelnuts, cacao powder, and chocolate, and stir to combine. Set aside.

Preheat the oven Preheat the oven to 350°F (180°C) and line a 9 × 13in (23 × 33cm) baking dish with parchment paper.

Assemble Melt the butter in a small saucepan over low heat. Begin by laying a sheet of phyllo pastry in your baking dish, then brush it generously with the melted butter. Top with another sheet and brush again. Repeat this process until you have layered 8 sheets of phyllo. Spread half of the filling mixture evenly over the layered sheets. Repeat the layering process with another 8 phyllo sheets, brushing each one with butter. Then spread the remaining filling mixture over the top. Finish with the remaining 8 phyllo sheets, again brushing each one with melted butter. Using a sharp knife, carefully cut the baklava into squares.

Bake Bake for 20–25 minutes or until the top achieves a golden-brown hue.

Prepare the syrup While the baklava bakes, combine the maple syrup with 1 cup (240ml) water in a saucepan. Bring to a boil, then reduce the heat to low and let it simmer for 10 minutes until you have a slightly reduced, sticky, pourable syrup. Remove from the heat and let it cool.

Pour As soon as the baklava is out of the oven, pour the prepared syrup evenly over it, ensuring each piece is well saturated. Allow the baklava to cool completely, letting the syrup fully soak in, before serving.

Storage Place the baklava pieces in an airtight container. They will stay fresh and delicious for 4–5 days. Enjoy!

Hazelnut Milk

Baklava

Almond Pulp Amaretti Cookies

If you make the almond milk on page 80, you can use the leftover pulp to make this recipe, which is not only incredibly easy but also extremely tasty! These amaretti cookies are crunchy on the outside and chewy on the inside, with a wonderful almond flavor. Amaretti are a must in an Italian kitchen—actually, in any kitchen. Serve them at any time, whether you want to impress your guests or just Netflix and chill!

Makes 20–24

Prep time 15 minutes, plus overnight drying

Cooking time 15 minutes

Ingredients

10z (300g) almond pulp left over from making almond milk (see p80)

¾ cup minus 2 tsp (140g) soft light brown sugar

1 tbsp baking powder

2 tbsp amaretto liqueur or almond essence

5 tbsp plus 1 tsp (80ml) aquafaba (liquid from canned chickpeas)

½ tsp lemon juice

Dry the almond pulp Spread out the leftover almond pulp on a baking sheet and let it dry out overnight. For a quicker method, you can dry it in the oven for 2–4 hours at the lowest possible setting, checking frequently to see if it's ready. Ensure the pulp is completely dry before using.

Blend the almond pulp Once dried, add the pulp to a blender and blend until fine. The blending process might release oils, making the pulp feel slightly moist. This is normal.

Prepare the dough In a mixing bowl, combine the blended almond pulp with the sugar and baking powder. In another bowl, whip the aquafaba and lemon juice until it forms soft peaks, similar to egg whites (we do this by hand, but you can use a hand mixer if you have one). Gently fold the aquafaba mixture into the dry ingredients. Add the amaretto liqueur or almond essence and mix until a dough forms.

Preheat the oven Preheat the oven to 350°F (180°C). Line a baking sheet with parchment paper.

Shape and bake Shape the dough into 20–24 small balls, placing them on the prepared baking sheet and spacing them slightly apart so they have room to expand. You can slightly flatten them if you prefer. Bake for about 15 minutes, or until the cookies are lightly golden.

Cool and serve Let the amaretti cool on the baking sheet for a few minutes, then transfer to a wire rack to cool completely.

Storage Store the amaretti in an airtight jar at room temperature. They will stay fresh for up to 2 weeks.

Almond Milk

Next time you are in a store, about to buy a super-expensive carton of plant-based milk, check the back of the box. Most of the time, you will see it is full of additives and chemical compounds to preserve the shelf life. Never fear—I will show you a super-easy way to get your own supply of fresh almond milk. Not only is it much cheaper, but you can also use the leftover pulp to make my delicious Almond Pulp Amaretti Cookies (see p79).

Makes 6–7 cups (1.4–1.7 liters)

Prep time 10-15 minutes, plus overnight soaking

Ingredients

2 cups (310g) raw almonds
6 cups (1.4 liters) water

- -

Soak the almonds Place the almonds in a large bowl and pour over enough water to cover them by about 1in (2.5cm). They will plump up as they absorb the water. Let soak for 8–12 hours, or overnight. This softens the almonds and makes them easier to blend.

Drain, rinse, and blend After soaking, drain and rinse the almonds under cool running water, then pour into a blender. Add the water and blend at the highest speed for 2 minutes. The almonds should be broken down into a very fine meal, and the liquid should be white and opaque.

Strain Line a large bowl with a nut-milk bag or piece of muslin. Pour the almond mixture into the bag or muslin. Close the bag or gather the ends of the muslin and squeeze well to extract as much almond milk as possible. You should be left with dry almond meal in the cloth and smooth almond milk in the bowl. Reserve the almond meal for use in another recipe.

Storage Store the almond milk in sealed bottles in the refrigerator. Shake well before using, as it may separate over time. Consume within 3-5 days for best quality and freshness.

Tiramisu

Tiramisu is one of my favorite desserts; it reminds me of Italy and my mom making it for our friends and family. This delicious plant-based version has nothing to envy in her original recipe.

Serves 6–8

Prep time 30 minutes, plus soaking and chilling time

Cooking time 25–30 minutes

Ingredients

For the sponge

5 tbsp plus 1 tsp (80ml) vegetable oil, plus extra for greasing

2 cups plus 2 tbsp (300g) all-purpose flour, plus extra for dusting

¾ cup plus 2 tbsp (180g) granulated sugar

1 tsp baking soda

pinch of salt

1 cup (200ml) soy milk

1 tbsp apple cider vinegar

For the cream

¾ cup (120g) cashews

14oz (400g) silken tofu

6½ tbsp (100ml) soy milk

2 tbsp lemon juice

To assemble

1¾ cups (400ml) strong coffee, made with used grounds and cooled

cocoa powder, for dusting

Soak the cashews Soak the cashews in a bowl of water for at least 2 hours.

Preheat the oven Preheat the oven to 400°F (200°C). Grease an 8in (20cm) square or round baking pan and dust with flour.

Mix the sponge batter In a large mixing bowl, whisk together the flour, granulated sugar, baking soda, and salt. In a separate bowl, combine the soy milk, vegetable oil, and apple cider vinegar.

Pour the wet ingredients into the dry ingredients, and mix until just combined. Be careful not to overmix.

Bake Pour the batter into the prepared pan and smooth the top. Bake for 20-25 minutes, or until a toothpick inserted into the center comes out clean.

Cool Allow the sponge to cool in the pan for 10 minutes before transferring to a wire rack to cool fully.

Prepare the cream Drain and rinse the soaked cashews then pour into a blender or food processor. Add the silken tofu, soy milk, and lemon juice. Blend until smooth and creamy. If the cream is too thick, add a little more soy milk until you reach your desired consistency.

Assemble Once the sponge cake is cool, cut it into ½in (1cm) slices. Tip the cooled coffee into a shallow bowl. Working quickly, dip a slice of the sponge cake into the coffee, ensuring it isn't soaked through. Place the dipped sponge slice in your chosen serving dish. Repeat until you have a single layer of coffee-dipped sponge slices arranged across the bottom of the dish. Spread a layer of the tofu-and-cashew cream over the top.

Repeat the process, alternating layers of coffee-dipped sponge slices and cream until you use up all the sponge and cream, finishing with a layer of cream on top.

Chill Cover the dish with biodegradable plastic wrap or a lid and refrigerate for at least 2 hours to allow the flavors to meld and the dessert to set.

Serve Just before serving, dust the top of the tiramisu with cocoa powder.

Storage Store leftovers in an airtight container in the refrigerator for 4–5 days. This dessert is best enjoyed fresh.

Pistachio Milk

The first time we made this milk, I didn't really know what to expect, because one of the main reasons I like pistachios is the crunch you get from every bite. However, it quickly became one of my favorite milks due to its incredible combo of sweet and savory flavors.

Makes 1 quart (1 liter)
Prep time 5 minutes

Ingredients
1 cup (140g) shelled pistachios
2 dates, pitted
4¼ cups (1 liter) water

- - - - - - - - - - - - - - - - -

Soak Place the pistachios in a bowl and pour over enough water to cover. Soak for at least 4 hours or overnight.

Blend Drain the soaked pistachios and add them to a blender along with the dates and water. Blend until smooth and creamy. If you wish, you can strain the pistachio milk through a nut-milk bag, muslin, or fine mesh sieve.

Storage Serve the pistachio milk immediately, or transfer it to a sealed container and refrigerate for up to 4 days. Shake well before using.

Pistachio Blondies

I guarantee you won't be able to resist the smell or flavor of these delicious blondies once you make them at home! The best thing is that you can make them using the leftover pulp from pistachio milk (see left).

Serves 12
Prep time 15 minutes
Cooking time 25–30 minutes

Ingredients
6 tbsp plant-based butter, melted, plus extra for greasing
1 tbsp milled flaxseed
1¼ cups (160g) gluten-free all-purpose flour
½ tsp baking powder
¾ cup (150g) soft light brown sugar
4 tbsp pure maple syrup
1 tsp grated lemon zest
2½oz (75g) pistachio pulp left over from making pistachio milk
handful of strawberries, finely chopped

- -

Preheat the oven Preheat the oven to 350°F (180°C). Grease an 8in (20cm) square baking pan and line with parchment paper.

Prepare the flax "egg" In a bowl, combine the milled flaxseed with 2 tablespoons water. Stir, then let it sit for a few minutes until it thickens to a gel-like consistency.

Mix the batter In a mixing bowl, whisk together the flour, baking powder, and sugar. Add the syrup and melted plant-based butter, along with the flax "egg" and lemon zest. Stir until combined. Gently fold in the leftover pistachio pulp and strawberries, carefully mixing until evenly distributed.

Bake Pour the batter into the prepared pan and spread it out evenly. Bake for 25–30 minutes, or until the blondies are set and the edges are lightly golden brown.

Cool and serve Let cool in the pan for about 10 minutes before transferring to a wire rack to cool completely, then enjoy.

Storage Store any leftover blondies in an airtight container at room temperature for up to 3 days, or in the refrigerator for up to 1 week. They can also be frozen for up to 2 months. Defrost thoroughly before serving.

Pistachio
Milk

Blondies

Black Sesame Seed Butter (Tahini)

If you are looking for a unique and flavorful butter, black sesame seed butter is definitely a great alternative to traditional nut butters, offering a distinctive nutty taste and rich color. You can spread it on bread or enrich the flavor of your next meal by dolloping it on top of soups or adding it to salads. You can even stir it through granola.

Makes 1 jar (about 250g)

Prep time 10 minutes
Cooking time 10 minutes

Ingredients

3¾ cups (500g) black sesame seeds

2-3 tsp olive oil (optional, for a smoother blend)

1 tsp salt or other flavorings of your choice (optional—you could try adding ground cinnamon or vanilla extract)

Preheat the oven Preheat the oven 230°F (120°C).

Roast the seeds The seeds are typically used as is, without needing to remove them from any pods, so simply spread out the seeds on a baking sheet in an even layer. Roast for about 5 minutes, then turn off the oven and leave them inside for an additional 5 minutes to ensure the seeds are well roasted but not burned.

Blend Transfer the roasted black sesame seeds to a food processor or blender. Add a drizzle of olive oil if you wish to help the blending process. Blend until the mixture reaches your desired consistency. For a smoother, more spreadable butter, add more oil.

Add flavoring (optional) You can add a pinch of salt or other flavorings if you wish. Blend again to mix in these additional flavors.

Storage Transfer the black sesame seed butter to a clean, airtight container. It will keep in the refrigerator for 2-3 weeks.

Homemade Mustard

Did you know you can easily make your own mustard from scratch? Mustard seeds, often overlooked in the spice cabinet, can be transformed into a tangy and flavorful condiment that adds a punch to any meal. This DIY mustard recipe is a nod to traditional methods, using simple ingredients to create something truly special. It's a must-try for anyone looking to enhance their culinary creations.

Makes 2 cups (450ml)
Prep time 5 minutes
Cooking time 10 minutes

Ingredients

1½ cups (145g) yellow mustard seeds
4 tbsp distilled white wine vinegar
½ tsp salt
¼ tsp ground turmeric
¼ tsp paprika
¼ tsp garlic powder
¼ tsp onion powder
⅛ tsp ground cinnamon
1 tbsp agave syrup

- -

Soak the mustard seeds Place the yellow mustard seeds in a bowl and cover them with 2½ cups (600ml) filtered water. Let soak for 4–6 hours or overnight.

Drain and rinse After soaking, drain the mustard seeds and rinse them thoroughly under cold water.

Blend In a blender or food processor, combine the soaked mustard seeds with the distilled wine vinegar, salt, turmeric, paprika, garlic powder, onion powder, ground cinnamon, and agave. Blend until smooth. If the mustard is too thick, add a splash of water until you reach your desired consistency.

Storage Transfer the homemade mustard to a clean airtight jar or container. Store it in the refrigerator for up to 2 weeks.

Sunflower Butter

Homemade sunflower butter is a delicious and nutritious alternative to traditional nut butters. It's made from the seeds of a sunflower head.

Makes 9oz (250g)

Prep time 30 minutes, plus 1 week drying time

Cooking time 10 minutes

Ingredients

1 sunflower head (with mature seeds)

2–3 tsp olive oil (optional, for a smoother blend)

1 tsp salt or other flavorings of your choice (optional—you could try adding ground cinnamon, cocoa powder, or vanilla extract)

Harvest and dry the sunflower head Cut the sunflower head from the stem when the seeds are fully mature and the sunflower is starting to die off. Leave it in a well-ventilated area to completely dry out; this might take a week or more.

Remove the seeds Once dry, gently pluck the seeds (kernels) from the sunflower head using your fingers or a fork.

Crush and soak Wrap the kernels in a clean kitchen towel or cloth and use a wooden rolling pin or mallet to gently crush them. This helps to open them up. Pour the crushed kernels into a bowl of water and let soak for about 30 minutes. The seeds will sink to the bottom. Scoop out and discard the floating kernels, then drain the seeds.

Preheat the oven Preheat the oven to 230°F (120°C).

Roast Spread out the seeds on a baking sheet in a single layer. Roast for about 5 minutes, then turn off the oven but leave them inside for another 5 minutes to ensure thorough roasting without burning.

Blend Transfer the roasted seeds to a food processor or blender. Add a drizzle of olive oil if you prefer a smoother consistency. Blend until it reaches your desired texture. More oil can be added for a thinner consistency.

Add flavoring (optional) You can add a pinch of salt or other flavorings if you wish. Blend again to mix in these additional flavors.

Storage Transfer the sunflower butter to a clean, airtight container. It will keep in the refrigerator for several weeks.

Variation: Pumpkin Seed Butter

» You can use the same method to make your own pumpkin seed butter: simply substitute the sunflower seeds for 2 cups (500g) pumpkin seeds and follow the steps above, starting at the roasting step (there's no need to soak).

» Pumpkin seeds, also known as pepitas, are rich in magnesium, zinc, omega-3 and omega-6 fatty acids, and antioxidants, making them beneficial for heart health and immune support, and giving them anti-inflammatory properties. Not only is this homemade pumpkin seed butter a delicious spread for bread and crackers, but it can also be used in salad dressings and sauces, or as a dip.

Crush

Soak

Blend

Store

88

Flowers

Nasturtiums

Nasturtium Vellutata 94
Nasturtium Butter 96
Pickled Nasturtium Seeds 96

Elderberry and Elderflower

Elderberry Syrup 97
Elderflower Cordial 99

Roses

Rose Powder 100
Rose and Raspberry Granita 100

Lavender

Lavender-Infused Oil 102

Calendula

Calendula-Infused Oil 104

Poppies

Poppy Seed Flower-Fetti Cake 105

Dandelions

Dandelion Honey 106

Nasturtium Vellutata

When you think about leaves, the first thing that comes to mind is probably a salad. But we are not making "boring" food here, and there are many other ways to put your nasturtium leaves to good use and extract that incredible flavor. If you've never heard of vellutata, this recipe not only explains how to make this delicious soup but also takes it to the next level with the creamiest and richest flavors. It might make you think, "I should have planted more nasturtiums!"

Serves 4

Prep time 10 minutes

Cooking time 20 minutes

Ingredients

4 tbsp olive oil

½ onion, diced

2 garlic cloves, minced

1 potato, diced

1 zucchini, diced

15-20 nasturtium leaves, washed, chopped, and dried

3 tbsp oat cream

2 cups (500ml) water

salt and freshly ground black pepper

To serve

fresh nasturtium flowers and young leaves

croutons or sliced bread

Sauté the vegetables Heat the oil in a large saucepan over medium heat. Add the onion and garlic, and sauté for 3-4 minutes until softened. Add the potato and zucchini, and cook for a few minutes more until they start to soften. Take the pan off the heat and let cool slightly.

Blend the soup Transfer the cooked vegetables to a blender. Add the nasturtium leaves, along with the oat cream, and blend until smooth. Gradually add the water, blending between each addition until smooth and velvety. Add more water if you prefer a more liquid consistency. Season with salt and pepper to taste.

Serve Ladle the vellutata into bowls. Top with fresh nasturtium flowers and young leaves, and serve with croutons or a slice of bread.

Storage Store any leftover vellutata in an airtight container in the refrigerator for up to 3 days.

Nasturtiums

» This incredible flower is a must-have in every garden. It grows quickly, and I often use it as a sacrificial plant in the garden to attract an array of pests, like the dreaded aphid. It masks the smell of your main crops, and once fully infested by pests, you can simply compost the entire plant. However, the main perk of having this plant is that every single part is edible. At first, when I tried it raw, I couldn't deal with the pungent, peppery flavor. However, if prepared correctly, using the recipes we've tried and tested over many years, you will be surprised by how versatile and delicious this plant can be.

Nasturtium Butter

Transform nasturtium flowers into this delicious, peppery spread. It is sure to impress your guests!

Makes about 9oz (250g)

Prep time 5 minutes

Ingredients

9oz (250g) plant-based butter,
  cubed

handful of nasturtium flowers,
  washed and dried

1 tsp finely chopped dill, parsley,
  chives, or sage (optional)

salt and freshly ground black
  pepper

Mix the ingredients In a bowl, combine the plant-based butter with the nasturtium flowers and herbs, if using. Mix to combine. Season with salt and pepper to taste.

Serve Serve with your favorite bread or crackers.

Storage Transfer the nasturtium butter to a clean airtight container and store in the refrigerator for up to a week.

Pickled Nasturtium Seeds

Pickled nasturtium seeds are a fantastic, homegrown alternative to traditional capers.

Makes 1 × 8oz (250ml) jar

Prep time 10 minutes, plus
soaking and pickling time

Cooking time 5 minutes

Ingredients

1 cup (300g) nasturtium seeds

fresh dill sprig (optional)

For the brine

1 cup (240ml) white vinegar

1 tablespoon salt

1 tablespoon caster sugar

1 teaspoon black peppercorns

2–3 garlic cloves, crushed

1 bay leaf

1 cup (240ml) water

Equipment

8oz (250ml) sterilized jar

Rinse and soak Rinse the nasturtium seeds in cold water, then soak overnight. Rinse again the next day.

Prepare the brine In a saucepan, combine the brine ingredients then bring to a boil, stirring to ensure the salt and sugar dissolve completely.

Pack the jar Pack the rinsed nasturtium seeds into a sterilized jar. Add the dill, if using, then pour in the hot pickling brine, ensuring the seeds are fully submerged. Leave about ½in (1cm) of space at the top of the jar. Seal and let cool.

Storage Store in the refrigerator. The flavor will develop over time and will be best after a week. Consume within 2 months.

Elderberry Syrup

Nature provides all we need in terms of food and natural remedies. You just need to learn where to look and how to use the many gifts she offers. Elderberry trees can be found in both the city and the countryside. They are best known for their flowers, but the flowers are not the only edible part. If you wait long enough after the flowering period, these trees will produce berries packed with immune-boosting properties. This homemade syrup is not only beneficial for your health but also deliciously sweet and versatile. There are two main varieties that are edible: *Sambucus nigra* (European elderberry) and *Sambucus canadensis* (American elderberry). They are both safe to eat when cooked. Do not eat these berries raw, as they contain cyanide, which is toxic. It gets destroyed during the cooking process.

Makes about 2 cups (450ml)

Prep time 15 minutes

Cooking time 45 minutes

Ingredients

2¼lb (1kg) elderberries

1 lemon, washed and sliced
   (peel on)

1 orange, washed and sliced
   (peel on)

1 cup (200g) soft light brown
   sugar

1–2 cinnamon sticks

Equipment

sterilized glass bottles or jars

Prepare the elderberries Remove the elderberries from their stems using a fork or your fingers. Rinse well in plenty of water, and discard any stems, leaves, or unripe berries.

Simmer In a large saucepan, combine the prepared elderberries with the lemon slices, orange slices, brown sugar, and cinnamon stick(s). Place over medium heat and bring the mixture to a simmer. Reduce the heat to low and let the syrup simmer gently for about 45 minutes, stirring occasionally.

Strain Remove the pot from the heat and let the syrup cool slightly, then strain into a clean container through a fine mesh sieve or piece of muslin to remove the solids. Press down on the fruit to extract as much liquid as possible.

Cool Let the elderberry syrup cool completely before transferring it to sterilized glass bottles or jars.

Serve Use the syrup as a sweet and tangy topping for pancakes, waffles, yogurt, or desserts. You can also dilute it with water or sparkling water to make a refreshing drink.

Storage Seal the bottles or jars tightly and store them in the refrigerator for to 2–3 weeks. Alternatively, you can freeze it in ice-cube trays for up to 6 months.

Elderflower Cordial

The elderflower is the sign of spring finally starting, and it fills the air with a sweet smell. The refreshing elderflower and lemon mocktail below brings back the sweet fragrance of childhood summers spent making cordial in the courtyard.

Makes 10 quarts (10 liters)

Prep time 10 minutes, plus cooling time and 1–5 days infusing time

Ingredients

10 quarts (10 liters) water

4 cups (800g) granulated sugar

14 large elderflower heads (each about the size of a palm)

zest and juice of 3–4 lemons

1½ tsp fresh yeast

Prepare the cordial base In a large pot, bring the water to a boil, then remove from heat. Add the sugar and stir until completely dissolved, creating a simple syrup. Let cool to room temperature.

Mix Gently rinse the elderflower heads to remove any dust or insects, handling them carefully to avoid losing the delicate blossoms. Place them in a large, clean bowl or container, along with the lemon zest and lemon juice. Pour the cooled syrup over the top and stir gently to mix. Sprinkle the fresh yeast over the mixture and stir gently once again.

Cover and infuse Cover the bowl with a clean cloth or biodegradable plastic wrap. Place it in a sunny spot that is sheltered from the rain, and leave to infuse. While the cordial is good after 24 hours, allowing it to brew for several days will mean it develops more complex flavors. Stir the mixture gently once or twice a day.

Strain After 1–2 days (or up to 5 days, if desired), strain the cordial through a fine mesh sieve or pieces of muslin and decant it into clean bottles or jars, discarding the elderflower heads and lemon zest.

Chill Refrigerate until chilled, and it's now ready to use.

Storage Store the elderflower cordial in the refrigerator for up to 2 weeks. For longer storage, freeze the cordial in ice-cube trays for up to 3 months. Thaw as needed.

~~~~~~~~~~~

Elderflower and Mint Mocktail

» Add some ice cubes to a glass, then pour in 2–3 tablespoons of your elderflower cordial. Top off with chilled sparkling water or lemonade.

» Garnish with fresh mint leaves and a slice of lemon for a refreshing touch and enjoy this delightful and elegant drink.

Rose Powder

I haven't given quantities here, as you can just work with as many rose petals as you're able to harvest.

Prep time 10 minutes, plus drying time

Ingredients

fresh rose petals (ensure they are organic and pesticide-free)

- - - - - - - - - - - - - - - - -

Harvest and clean Harvest your organic rose petals and gently clean them.

Air-dry Arrange the clean petals in a single layer on a baking sheet and leave to air-dry until crisp. This could take 4–5 days.

Grind Using a pestle and mortar or spice grinder, grind the dried petals into a fine powder. Sift through a fine mesh sieve for a smoother texture (optional).

Storage Store the petal powder in an airtight container away from sunlight. It will keep for 3–6 months.

Rose and Raspberry Granita

You can use rose petals to make an elegant dessert that's as simple as it is sophisticated. The sweet scent of roses and the rich color of raspberries make this granita a true showstopper.

Serves 4
Prep time 20 minutes, plus 4–6 hours freezing

Ingredients

handful of fresh rose petals (preferably red or dark pink for the best color), plus extra to serve
2½ cups (600ml) water
½ cup (100g) granulated sugar
½ cup (120ml) fresh raspberry juice (homemade or store-bought)
fresh raspberries, to serve

- -

Prepare the rose petals Gently rinse the rose petals under cool water to remove any dirt or residue, then set aside.

Make the infusion Bring the water to a boil in a saucepan, then take off the heat. Add the rose petals and allow them to steep in the hot water for 10–15 minutes to extract their color and fragrance. The water should turn a light pink.

Strain and sweeten Strain the rose-infused water through a fine mesh sieve into a bowl to remove the petals. Add the sugar while the water is still warm, and stir until the sugar is completely dissolved.

Add the raspberry juice Pour the raspberry juice into the sweetened rose water, and mix well to combine the flavors.

Freeze and scrape Pour the mixture into a shallow, freezer-proof container. A shallow dish helps the granita freeze more evenly and quickly. Freeze for 1–2 hours, then use a fork to scrape and stir the mixture to break up any ice crystals. Return to the freezer. Continue to scrape the granita every 30 minutes until the mixture is fully frozen and has a fluffy, crystalline texture. This usually takes 4–6 hours.

Serve Once the granita is fully frozen and has a snowlike texture, use a fork to fluff it up and scoop it into serving glasses. Garnish with additional fresh rose petals or a few fresh raspberries for a beautiful presentation.

Storage Store any leftover granita in the freezer for up to 3 months. Before serving, scrape it with a fork to restore its fluffy texture.

Lavender-Infused Oil

We grow an astonishing diversity of flowers in our garden to welcome wildlife and pollinators. Not only does this provide us with a natural source of pest control, but it also allows us to mimic nature and ensure that everything remains in balance. We've used lavender for this recipe, but you can create this oil using many kinds of dried flowers, infusing your favorite carrier oil with their scent and beneficial properties. It's a wonderful way to nurture your body, and the process is as easy as harvesting the flowers. You can use this lavender-infused oil for skin and hair care or in edible recipes, depending on the base oil used.

Makes 9fl oz (250ml)

Prep time 15 minutes, plus 4–6 weeks for infusion

Ingredients

½ cup (8 tbsp) dried organic lavender flowers (see Drying lavender, below)

9fl oz (250ml) bottle of your favorite organic oil (e.g., cold-pressed sunflower oil)

Equipment

sterilized jar

9fl oz (250ml) sterilized bottle

Prepare the infusion Place the dried lavender flowers in the sterilized jar. Pour over your chosen oil, ensuring the flowers are fully submerged.

Seal and infuse Close the jar tightly and shake gently to mix. Store in a cool, dark place for 4–6 weeks to infuse. The longer you give it, the stronger the scent and properties of the lavender will be.

Strain After the infusion period, strain the oil through a piece of muslin into a sterilized bottle or jar. Discard the lavender flowers (you can compost them or dry them out in the sun to use for scented pouches). Label and seal the bottle or jar.

Storage Store the strained oil in a cool, dark place. It will keep for up to a year.

Drying lavender

» To dry your flowers, harvest them in bunches, then hang them upside down in a warm, well-ventilated room until fully dry. We hang them in our kitchen, and the drying usually takes a few days. Ensure your flowers are completely dried before making the infusion, as fresh flowers can introduce moisture, leading to spoilage.

Calendula-Infused Oil

Calendula has strong anti-inflammatory and antimicrobial benefits. This oil can be used for skincare, hair treatments, or in culinary preparations, depending on the base oil's suitability.

Makes 9fl oz (250ml)

Prep time 15 minutes, plus 4–6 weeks for infusion

Ingredients

½ cup dried organic calendula flowers (see Drying calendula, below)

9fl oz (250ml) bottle of your favorite organic oil (e.g., cold-pressed sunflower or olive oil)

Equipment

sterilized jar

9fl oz (250ml) sterilized bottle

Prepare the infusion Place the dried calendula flowers in the sterilized jar. Pour the oil over the flowers until they are fully submerged.

Seal and infuse Close the jar tightly and shake gently to mix. Store in a cool, dark place for 4–6 weeks to infuse. The longer you give it, the stronger the scent and properties of the calendula will be.

Strain After the infusion period, strain the oil through a piece of muslin into a sterilized bottle or jar. Discard the calendula flowers (you can compost them or dry them out in the sun to use for scented pouches). Label and seal the bottle or jar.

Storage Store in a cool, dark place. It will keep for up to a year.

Drying calendula

» Calendula can be dried overnight in a dehydrator on the lowest setting (usually 100°F/40°C). If you don't have a dehydrator, you can let it dry out naturally on a flat surface, but it will take 3–7 days depending on your local climate.

Poppy Seed Flower-Fetti Cake

Two of Iasmina's favorite things, flowers and cake, combined in this beautiful twist on a funfetti cake, packed with poppy seeds and flavor.

Serves 8–10

Prep time 30 minutes, plus cooling and decorating

Cooking time 30–35 minutes

Ingredients

plant-based butter, for greasing

2¾ cups (350g) all-purpose flour, plus extra for dusting

2¾ cups (270g) granulated sugar

½ tsp baking powder

½ tsp baking soda

⅓ cup (60g) poppy seeds

⅓ tsp salt

½ cup (120ml) coconut oil or olive oil

1½ cups (350ml) soy milk

2 tbsp apple cider vinegar

5 tbsp lemon juice

For the buttercream

1 cup (16 tbsp) edible flower petals, plus extra to serve

4oz (115g) plant-based butter

4 cups (550g) powdered sugar

3 tbsp lemon juice

Preheat the oven Preheat the oven to 400°F (200°C). Grease and flour two 8in (20cm) round cake pans.

Mix the batter In a large bowl, whisk together the flour, sugar, baking powder, baking soda, poppy seeds, and salt. In a separate bowl, whisk together the coconut oil (or olive oil), soy milk, apple cider vinegar, and lemon juice. Pour the wet ingredients into the dry ingredients and mix until just combined. Avoid overmixing; just stir until the batter is smooth.

Bake Divide the batter evenly between the prepared cake pans. Bake for 30–35 minutes, or until a toothpick inserted into the center comes out clean.

Cool Allow the cakes to cool in the pans for 10 minutes, then transfer to a wire rack to cool completely before frosting.

Prepare the buttercream Gently wash and pat dry the edible flower petals, then finely chop.

In a medium bowl, beat the plant-based butter with a hand mixer until creamy and smooth. Gradually add the powdered sugar, beating on low speed until fully incorporated. Add the lemon juice and mix until smooth and fluffy, then gently fold the chopped flower petals into the frosting.

Assemble and decorate the cake If needed, level the tops of the cakes with a knife to ensure they are flat. Spread a layer of buttercream on top of one cake layer. Place the second cake layer on top and cover the top and sides of the cake with the remaining buttercream.

Serve Sprinkle additional flower petals on top or around the edges for a beautiful floral touch before serving.

Storage The cake will keep at room temperature for up to 2 days. For longer storage, keep the cake in the refrigerator for up to a week. Allow it to come to room temperature before serving. The cake can also be frozen (uniced) for up to 3 months. Wrap it tightly in biodegradable plastic wrap and foil before freezing. Thaw in the refrigerator overnight before serving.

Dandelion Honey

Dandelion "honey" is our favorite vegan alternative to traditional honey. Derived from dandelion flowers, this healthy floral syrup boasts antioxidant properties and supports digestion. Not only is it kinder to bees, but the process of making it is also engaging, enjoyable, and affordable. Enjoy it as a sweetener over pancakes or spread on toast.

Makes about 1–1½ cups (240–350ml)

Prep time 20 minutes

Cooking time 1½ –2½ hours

Ingredients

2 cups (100g) dandelion flower heads

1½ cups (350ml) water

2 slices of organic lemon

superfine sugar (quantity depends on the liquid obtained)

Equipment

sterilized jar with a snug-fitting lid

- -

Harvest and clean Start by gathering your fresh dandelion flowers from your garden or local park (ensure they are free from any pesticides or chemical sprays). To ensure they're free from insects, immerse the petals in cold water for about 5 minutes, then strain.

Prepare the infusion Place the cleaned dandelion flower heads in a saucepan and pour in the water. Add the lemon slices and place the saucepan over high heat. Bring to a boil, then reduce the heat to low and simmer for 15 minutes to infuse the dandelion essence into the water.

Steep overnight After simmering, remove the saucepan from the heat. Cover and steep overnight to ensure a stronger flavor.

Strain and measure The next day, strain the mixture through a piece of muslin or a fine mesh strainer into a bowl, pressing the petals to extract all the liquid. Measure the weight of the resulting liquid, then measure the same weight of sugar.

Make the "honey" Return the liquid to the saucepan, incorporating the measured sugar. Place over medium heat and stir gently until the sugar dissolves, then bring the mixture to a gentle boil. Simmer for about 15 minutes until the mixture achieves a honeylike consistency, then take it off the heat.

Storage Pour your dandelion honey into the sterilized jar and seal tightly. Store in a cool, dark place. Homemade dandelion honey, when stored properly, can last for up to 6 months. Over time, the flavor may change, or it may crystallize, much like regular honey.

Prepare the infusion

Strain and measure

Extract the liquid

Make the honey

Fruit

Zucchini

Stuffed Zucchini 113
Deep-Fried Zucchini Flowers 114
Leaves and Stems Pesto 114

Cucumber

Tzatziki 117
Cucumber Juice Mocktail 117

Eggplants

Eggplant Parmigiana 118
Salata de Vinete (Eggplant Dip) 120

Tomatoes

Tomato Skin Powder 121
Green Tomato Chutney 122

Corn

Grilled Polenta with Sage 124
Corn Pancakes 128
Corn Silk Tea 129

Apples

Apple Kombucha 130
Apple Strudel 132
Fruit Leather 133

Pineapple

Pineapple Chutney 136
Pineapple Tepache 138

Strawberries

Dehydrated Strawberries 139
Strawberry Cheong 140

Lemons

Preserved Lemon Peel 143
Purple Lemonade 143

Oranges

Candied Chocolate Orange Peel 144
Whole Orange Almond Cake 146

Plums

Găluște cu Prune (Plum Dumplings) 148

Figs

Fig Panna Cotta 149
Green Fig Syrup 150
Stuffed Figs 150

Dates

Date Bites 153
Date Seed Coffee 153

Stuffed Zucchini

This is one of my favorite recipes prepared by my mom, but instead of using tuna as she does, I have added my own twist, making a plant-based version, which is just as great as the original recipe. We sometimes use marrows to create this recipe; a marrow is simply an overgrown zucchini (perhaps because you forgot to harvest it!). Contrary to the common opinion, overgrown doesn't equal tasteless, especially if grown organically.

Serves 4

Prep time 20 minutes
Cooking time 50-60 minutes

Ingredients

4 tbsp olive oil
2 red onions, finely chopped
4 garlic cloves, finely chopped
1 cup (200g) amaranth or quinoa
1-2 cups (240-480ml) water
1 cup (150g) peas
2 large zucchini
herbs or spices of your choice
    (optional)
salt and freshly ground black
    pepper

To serve
arugula leaves
sesame seeds
chopped herbs of your choice
tomatoes

Preheat the oven Preheat the oven to 350°F (180°C).

Sauté the onions and garlic Heat the olive oil in a skillet over medium heat. Add the onions and garlic, and sauté for 5-10 minutes until golden, stirring occasionally.

Cook the amaranth/quinoa Add the amaranth or quinoa to the pan and pour over 1-2 cups (240-480ml) water—this will vary depending on the size of your pan, but it should be enough to cover the grains by ½-¾in (1-2cm). Cook for 10 minutes.

Add the peas and seasonings Add the peas and any preferred herbs or spices. Season with salt and pepper, and cook for another 20 minutes, adding extra water if needed.

Stuff the zucchini Halve the zucchini lengthwise and scoop out the flesh from the middle (reserve the pulp to use in another recipe—it will keep for 3-5 days in the refrigerator and can be added to pasta sauces, etc). Spoon the filling mixture into the hollowed-out zucchini.

Bake Bake for 30-40 minutes until golden.

Serve Serve on a bed of arugula, garnished with sesame seeds and chopped herbs, with tomatoes on the side.

Storage Refrigerate in an airtight container and consume within 2-3 days.

Deep-Fried Zucchini Flowers

If you grow zucchini, try harvesting a few of the male flowers. Stuff them with delicious plant-based ricotta and deep-fry them for a pure explosion of flavor. Male flowers are long with a thin stem and open only in the morning, while female flowers have an immature zucchini at the base. Always leave some male flowers so pollinators can pollinate your plants and to produce zucchini.

Serves 5 (2 flowers each)

Prep time 15 minutes

Cooking time 10 minutes

Ingredients

about 1 portion Plant-
Based Ricotta
(see p164)

10 zucchini flowers

vegetable oil, for
deep-frying

For the tempura batter

1 cup (130g) all-purpose
flour

¾ cup (100g) cornstarch

1 tsp baking powder

½ tsp garlic granules

½ tsp paprika (optional)

salt and freshly ground
black pepper

1¾ cups (400ml) water

To serve

finely grated lemon zest

your favorite fresh herbs

Equipment

piping bag

Fill the flowers Fill the piping bag with plant-based ricotta and carefully pipe it into the zucchini flowers.

Prepare the batter In a large bowl, combine the tempura batter ingredients to form a smooth batter.

Batter and fry Pour the oil into a deep-sided skillet to a depth of 2in (5cm) and place over medium heat. The oil is hot enough for frying when a small amount of batter dropped into the pan sizzles and floats. Dip the filled flowers into the tempura batter, then carefully transfer them to the hot oil, working in batches to avoid overcrowding. Fry for a few minutes until golden and crispy, then remove with a slotted spoon and set aside on a plate lined with paper towels.

Serve Serve hot, garnished with lemon zest and your chosen herbs. These are best enjoyed fresh.

Leaves and Stems Pesto

Did you know that you can eat the young stems and leaves of zucchini plants? Just be careful not to use leaves affected by powdery mildew.

Serves 4

Prep time 10 minutes

Ingredients

4–5 young zucchini leaves
and stems

½ cup (80g) pine nuts

½ cup (120ml) olive oil,
plus extra as needed

2 garlic cloves, peeled

salt and freshly ground
black pepper

Prepare the leaves and stems Peel the stems to remove any spikes. Wash the leaves and stems.

Blend the pesto Add all the ingredients to a food processor. Blend, adding more olive oil as needed to achieve the desired consistency. Season with salt and pepper to taste.

Serve Use as a dip or a topping for your favorite meal.

Storage Store in an airtight container in the refrigerator and use within 3–4 days.

Leaves and Stems Pesto

Deep-Fried Zucchini Flowers

Cucumber Juice Mocktail

Tzatziki

Tzatziki

For me, there's nothing better than making a zero-waste recipe that uses whole fruits in a single dish. Tzatziki is a delicious, refreshing dip that we serve almost every time we have friends over for dinner. It looks stunning alongside flatbread as an appetizer and makes a great dip for vegetables or falafel. It takes just 15 minutes to whip up this incredible recipe.

Makes 2 cups (450ml)

Prep time 15 minutes

Ingredients

1 large cucumber

9oz (250g) plant-based Greek yogurt

3 garlic cloves, minced

1 tbsp olive oil

1 tbsp lemon juice or apple cider vinegar

1 tbsp finely chopped herbs (such as dill, mint, or parsley)

salt and freshly ground black pepper

- -

Grate the cucumber Grate the cucumber using a box grater or a food processor, then transfer to a fine mesh sieve or a clean kitchen towel and press out the excess moisture into a bowl. Reserve the drained liquid in case you need it later, or to use in another recipe (see right).

Mix In a mixing bowl, combine the squeezed grated cucumber with the yogurt, garlic, olive oil, lemon juice or vinegar, and chopped herbs. Season with salt and pepper to taste. If the tzatziki is too thick, you can add a little bit of the reserved cucumber liquid to reach your desired consistency.

Chill Cover with biodegradable plastic wrap or transfer the tzatziki to an airtight container and refrigerate for at least 1 hour.

Serve Serve with your chosen accompaniments.

Storage Store any leftover tzatziki in an airtight container in the refrigerator for up to 3 days

Cucumber Juice Mocktail

A delicious way to use up any leftover cucumber juice you might have after making tzatziki and similar recipes. This refreshing treat is perfect for enjoying on a hot day.

Serves 2

Prep time 10 minutes

Ingredients

1 cup (240ml) cucumber juice

handful of fresh mint leaves, plus extra to serve

4 tbsp lime juice

4 tbsp simple syrup, or to taste (see below)

4 tbsp sparkling water

ice cubes

cucumber slices, to serve

- -

Blend and strain Add the cucumber juice and mint leaves to a blender and blend, then strain into a pitcher through a fine mesh sieve.

Mix Add the lime juice and simple syrup and stir well to combine.

Serve Fill two glasses with ice cubes and pour over the cucumber mixture. Top off with the sparkling water, and garnish each glass with a mint leaf and a few cucumber slices.

Simple syrup

» Combine 4 tablespoons each of sugar and water in a small saucepan. Heat until the sugar dissolves completely. Cool before use.

Eggplant Parmigiana

Eggplant parmigiana is a staple in every Italian kitchen, and any time I knew my grandma was making it for lunch, I would pester my mom to take me to her house as soon as she could. I used to love going to the local farmers' market with her and picking up fresh ingredients to make this mouthwatering dish. I've created my own version based on her recipe but with a plant-based twist that has nothing to envy in the original version.

Serves 4

Prep time 15 minutes

Cooking time 30 minutes

Ingredients

4 eggplants, sliced into ¼in (5mm) slices

4–6 tbsp olive oil

3 garlic cloves

1 onion

3 large tomatoes, chopped

10oz (300g) tomato purée

1 tsp dried oregano

1lb 2oz (500g) plant-based mozzarella

1lb 2oz (500g) plant-based Parmesan cheese

handful of basil leaves

salt and freshly ground black pepper

Preheat the oven Preheat the oven to 350°F (180°C).

Grill the eggplants Preheat the grill to medium. Lay the eggplant slices in a baking sheet and grill for a few minutes on each side until tender and lightly charred. You'll need to work in batches. Set aside.

Prepare the sauce Heat the olive oil in a saucepan over medium heat. Add the garlic and onion and sauté for 4–5 minutes until fragrant, then stir in the chopped tomatoes, tomato purée and oregano. Season to taste with salt and pepper, then simmer for 15–20 minutes until the sauce is slightly reduced and the tomatoes are soft.

Assemble Arrange a third of the grilled eggplant slices in the base of a 9 × 13in (23 × 33cm) baking dish. Top with a third of the tomato sauce, then add a third of the plant-based mozzarella and a third of the plant-based Parmesan cheese, and sprinkle over some basil leaves. Repeat the layers twice more until all the ingredients are used up, finishing with a layer of cheese on top.

Bake Bake for 20 minutes or until the cheese is melted and bubbly, then serve.

Storage Store any leftovers in an airtight container in the refrigerator for up to 3 days.

Salata de Vinete (Eggplant Dip)

This dish, introduced to me by Iasmina, is a traditional dip (or salad) that also happens to be plant-based. It's like baba ghanoush. During eggplant season, her family gathers for a festive grilling session, turning dozens of eggplants into this mouthwatering delight! They prepare enough jars to last for months, enjoying it daily as a side or dip. It's so irresistibly delicious that we often spread it on a slice of bread for breakfast.

Makes about 2 cups (500g)
Prep time 15 minutes
Cooking time 30–40 minutes

Ingredients

4 small to medium eggplants
2 garlic cloves, minced
½ onion, diced
2 handfuls of flat-leaf parsley, finely chopped, plus extra to serve
juice of ½ lemon
1 tbsp plant-based mayonnaise (optional)
olive oil, for drizzling
sea salt and freshly ground black pepper

Char the eggplants If you have a gas range, the easiest way to do this is to place the eggplants directly on the gas stove grates and cook for 10–15 minutes, turning occasionally using tongs, until the skin is charred and the flesh becomes soft. Alternatively, you can roast them in an oven preheated to 375°F (190°C) for 30 minutes.

Peel the eggplants Once the eggplants are charred and softened, transfer them to a colander set over a bowl so any excess liquid can drain away. Let them cool slightly, then peel off the charred skin and discard.

Mash and mix Transfer the peeled eggplant flesh to a mixing bowl. Use a fork or potato masher to mash until smooth, then add the garlic, onion, parsley, lemon juice, and mayo (if using). Season with salt and pepper, and mix well to combine all the ingredients evenly. Taste and adjust the seasoning as needed, adding more salt, pepper, or lemon juice according to your preferences.

Serve Transfer the salata de vinete to a serving dish. Finish with a drizzle of olive oil and additional chopped parsley. Serve with bread, crackers, or vegetable crudités.

Storage Store any leftovers in an airtight container in the refrigerator for 3–4 days—the flavors may intensify over time. Make sure to stir well before serving.

Tomato Skin Powder

When I was a kid, I used to hate finding small bits of tomato peel in my plates of pasta and ragù, but over the years, my taste buds developed—and now I've found a really cool way to use those peels for the most delicious condiment. This powder can be used as a seasoning or a marinade ingredient to add an extra kick of flavor to any meal. Scale the ingredients up or down depending on the quantity of tomato skins you have.

Makes 1 jar (about 1¼ cups/300g)

Prep time 20 minutes

Cooking time 20-24 hours in a dehydrator or 4-5 hours in an oven

Ingredients

2¼lb (1kg) tomato skins

1 tsp garlic powder

1 tsp dried oregano

1 tsp dried basil

Equipment

dehydrator (optional)

Dry the skins Spread out the skins on a baking sheet or dehydrating tray. Dry out in a very low oven (170-200°F/95-110°C) for approximately 4-5 hours, in a dehydrator set to 104°F (40°C) for approximately 20-24 hours, or under the sun (weather permitting) until fully dried. All these timings are guidelines only—whichever method you use, you will need to check back periodically, and continue until the skins have fully dried out.

Blend Add the dried skins to a blender with the garlic powder, oregano, and basil, and blend to a fine powder.

Storage Keep in an airtight container in a cool, dry place for up to 3 months.

Green Tomato Chutney

My grandma used to be a fan of green tomatoes straight from the plant, enjoyed with just a sprinkle of salt. I'm not that brave, but I still find them delightful if prepared in the right way. You can pair this delicious chutney with almost anything; all my neighbors end up with a jar at the end of the year.

Makes 6–8 cups (1.5–2 liters)
Prep time 30 minutes
Cooking time 1½–2 hours

Ingredients

5 tbsp olive oil
2 onions, finely chopped
6 garlic cloves, minced
6 medium green tomatoes, chopped
3 apples, cored and chopped
3½oz (100g) fresh ginger, minced
2⅔ cups Demerara sugar
1¼ cups (300ml) vinegar (apple cider or white wine vinegar work well)
juice of 4 oranges
1 tsp salt
7oz (200g) Thai basil, chopped

Equipment

3–4 sterilized 16fl oz (500ml) jars with lids

- -

Cook the aromatics Heat the olive oil in a large, heavy-based saucepan over medium heat. Add the onions and garlic, and sauté for 5–10 minutes until they become soft and translucent.

Add the fruits and ginger Add the chopped green tomatoes, apples, and minced ginger to the saucepan. Cook for about 10 minutes, stirring occasionally, until the fruits start to soften.

Stir and simmer Stir in the sugar, vinegar, orange juice, and salt. Bring to a boil, then reduce the heat to low and simmer gently for 1½–2 hours, stirring occasionally. The chutney should thicken and reduce. A few minutes before the end of the cooking time, stir in the Thai basil (you don't want to add it too early, as you want the herb to remain fresh and aromatic).

Test for doneness The chutney is ready when it has a thick, jamlike consistency. You can test its readiness by dragging a spoon through the mixture; it should leave a trail that doesn't fill in quickly.

Bottle the chutney While still hot, carefully ladle the chutney into the sterilized jars. Seal the jars while hot to ensure a good seal.

Storage Store the chutney in a cool, dark place. It will last for several months. Once opened, keep refrigerated and consume within 1 month.

Grilled Polenta with Sage

My grandpa was fond of making polenta, and we always ended up with some leftovers as he liked to cook massive batches for family and guests. The day after making the polenta, he used to slice it and grill it over an open fire, giving it a smoky, crispy crust.

Serves 4–6
Prep time 10 minutes
Cooking time 30–40 minutes, plus cooling time

Ingredients
4¼ cups (1 liter)
½ vegetable stock cube
1 cup (200g) polenta
1 tsp salt
3 tbsp chopped sage leaves
vegetable oil, for brushing
freshly ground black pepper

Tip
» This polenta can also be enjoyed straight out of the pan as a creamy polenta. Simply skip the chilling and grilling steps and serve it directly from the saucepan or after letting it cool slightly to thicken.

Cook the polenta In a large saucepan, bring the water to a boil. Add the half stock cube and stir to dissolve, then gradually add the polenta, whisking all the while to avoid lumps. Reduce the heat to low and cook, stirring frequently, for 20–25 minutes, or until the polenta thickens and pulls away from the sides of the pan. Stir in the salt and chopped sage, and season with black pepper to taste. Mix well.

Cool Transfer the cooked polenta to a lightly greased or parchment paper-lined baking dish. Smooth the top with a spatula. Let cool completely and firm up. You can speed this up by placing it in the refrigerator for about 1 hour.

Slice and grill Once the polenta has set and is firm, cut it into your desired shapes (slices, squares, or triangles). Preheat the grill to medium-high or place a griddle pan over medium-high heat.

Grill Lightly brush each polenta piece with vegetable oil, then grill for 2–4 minutes on each side until grill marks appear and the polenta is warm and crispy.

Serve Serve warm. This polenta can be enjoyed as a side dish or with your favorite dipping sauces.

Storage Store leftover grilled polenta in an airtight container in the refrigerator for up to 4 days. Reheat on the grill or in a skillet with a little oil to restore its crispiness.

Light the fire with corn
» I love to cook this polenta outside over a fire or barbecue. If you're ever cooking outside using fresh corn, did you know you can use the cobs as your cooking fuel? Once you've removed the kernels from the cobs, the stripped cobs can be burned in an outdoor fire or barbecue.

Preparing the fire

Lighting the fire

Slice

Grill

126

Corn Pancakes

When I was a kid, I remember our house being surrounded by endless fields of corn, and one of the best games was running through them with friends, even though they were full of insects that stuck to our shirts and hair. And I used to love coming home to my grandma's place and smelling the sweet, delicious aroma of corn pancakes from the entrance, ready for me and my friends to enjoy. We would savor them while listening to the sounds of cicadas and retreat to the basement to seek relief from the scorching summer heat. Serve these with your choice of toppings—they're great with maple syrup, fresh fruit, or plant-based yogurt.

Serves 4

Prep time 10 minutes

Cooking time 15 minutes

Ingredients

1¾–2¾ cups corn kernels (depending on how dense you like your batter)

2–3 tbsp agave syrup

1/2 cup (120ml) water

2 tbsp olive oil

- -

Prepare the corn kernels If using fresh corn, remove the kernels from the cob. If using canned or frozen corn, ensure it's drained and thawed if necessary.

Make the batter In a blender or food processor, combine the corn kernels, agave syrup, and water. Blend until smooth.

Cook Heat the olive oil in a nonstick skillet over medium heat. Pour about 4 tablespoons of the batter into the heated pan for each pancake. Cook until bubbles form on the surface, then flip and cook until golden brown on both sides. Set aside on a plate to keep warm and repeat the process with the remaining batter, adding more olive oil to the pan if needed.

Serve Serve warm with all your favorite toppings.

Storage Store any leftover pancakes in an airtight container in the refrigerator for up to 3 days.

Corn
Silk Tea

Corn silk, when brewed into tea, offers a mild, slightly sweet flavor. It's known for its anti-inflammatory and diuretic properties (it's sometimes used to help ease the symptoms of UTIs). I used to just harvest the corn and discard the silks into the compost, but then I read about this famous practice in Mexico, and I gave it a go. During corn season, you can dry out the silks, then store in a jar and use for this incredible natural remedy.

Makes 1 small jar
Prep time 10 minutes

Ingredients
5–10 corn cob silks

Equipment
dehydrator (optional)

- -

Prepare the corn silks Clean the corn silks, ensuring they are free of debris.

Dry To use a dehydrator, spread the corn silks in a single layer on a dehydrator tray. Dry out at 95–114°F (35–46°C) for 1–4 hours, checking back periodically. The corn silk is fully dehydrated when it feels brittle and snaps easily. There should be no visible moisture. Drying at a low temperature helps preserve the flavor and nutritional qualities. Alternatively, you can dry the silks in the sun or at room temperature by spreading them out in a single layer and leaving for a few days until fully dry.

Grind Once dry, grind the corn silk into a fine powder in a blender or using a pestle and mortar.

Storage Store in an airtight container in a cool, dry place away from direct sunlight. It will keep for about 4 months.

Brewing the tea

» Place 1–2 teaspoons of corn silk powder in a cup or infuser. Pour over some boiling water and steep for 10–15 minutes. Strain if needed and enjoy.

Apple Kombucha

For me and my fiancée Iasmina, choosing fermented drinks as part of our lifestyle has been a revelation. Much like fermented foods, these beverages don't just offer the sheer joy of consumption; they also hold a unique power. Kombucha, which is rich in beneficial probiotics, is crafted using a SCOBY (symbiotic culture of bacteria and yeast). These are easy to source online and from some health food stores. Thanks to the beneficial bacteria found in kombucha, our gut health and food digestion have noticeably improved. We've both felt a more robust immune response, fewer dietary intolerances, and an overall boost in our well-being and health.

Makes about 2 quarts (2 liters)

Prep time 20 minutes
First fermentation 7–10 days
Second fermentation 5–7 days

Ingredients

2 quarts (2 liters) filtered water
4–5 tsp (16g) loose black tea leaves (see opposite)
½ cup (120g) superfine sugar
2 SCOBYs
2½–4¼ cups (600ml–1 liter) apple juice

Equipment

2½-quart (2.5-liter) sterilized glass jar
sterilized round, clip-top, pressure-safe glass bottle

Prepare the tea Bring the filtered water to a boil, then pour it into a jug and add the tea leaves to brew. Add the sugar while the tea is still warm, and ensure it dissolves completely. Let the tea cool to room temperature.

Add the SCOBYs Ensure that the tea is entirely cold before introducing your SCOBYs to prevent harming them. Strain the cold tea into your sterilized jar and add both SCOBYs. Cover the jar with a paper towel or muslin cloth, and secure with an elastic band or string.

First fermentation Let ferment at room temperature in a dark place like a pantry for 7–10 days.

Second fermentation After the first phase, add the apple juice and stir to combine, then transfer your SCOBYs to a "SCOBY hotel," along with 1 cup (240ml) of the liquid (see below) and pour the remaining liquid into the bottles for the second fermentation, leaving the top third to half of each bottle empty, so there is space for the liquid to bubble. Let ferment at room temperature for another 5–7 days. Remember to "burp" (open) your bottles every day to release the built-up gas.

Storage Once fermentation is complete, store the brewed kombucha in the refrigerator, where it will keep for up to a month.

~~~~~~~~~

SCOBY hotel

» Use an extra jar to store your SCOBYs between brews; this is known as the "SCOBY hotel." Pour over enough of the brewed kombucha from the first fermentation to cover the SCOBYs (about 1 cup/240ml), and keep at room temperature. I've kept a SCOBY in the "hotel" for as long as 6–12 months.

Teas to use for kombucha

» BLACK TEA
This is the most traditional and commonly used tea for kombucha. Black tea provides a robust flavor and plenty of nutrients for the SCOBY.

» GREEN TEA
This offers a lighter, more delicate flavor. Green tea is rich in antioxidants and gives the kombucha a fresher, crisper taste.

» OOLONG TEA
A middle ground between black and green tea, oolong offers a more complex flavor profile and is also rich in nutrients.

» WHITE TEA
This is less processed than other teas and can create a very delicate kombucha with subtle flavors.

» YERBA MATE
Known for its energizing properties, yerba mate can be used to bring a different twist to your kombucha. It can be more challenging to use, so it's typically recommended for more experienced brewers.

» COMBINATIONS
Often, brewers will blend different teas to achieve specific flavor profiles. For example, a mix of black and green teas is quite popular.

Teas to avoid

» HERBAL AND FLAVORED
These can contain oils and additives that might harm the SCOBY. However, once you have a strong and healthy SCOBY, you can experiment with herbal teas in small batches.

» DECAFFEINATED
The decaffeination process removes some of the nutrients that the SCOBY needs to thrive.

Apple Strudel

I tried this recipe for the first time at Iasmina's house in Italy, and I was blown away by the amazing flavor. I had eaten strudel many times in the past, but nothing compared to this recipe! Serve it with plant-based vanilla ice cream for a sweet finish.

Serves 6–8
Prep time 30 minutes
Cooking time 30–35 minutes

Ingredients
10–12 small to medium apples (such as Gala or Golden Delicious), peeled, cored, and grated

½ tsp ground cinnamon
1 tbsp ground semolina
10½oz (320g) sheet plant-based ready-rolled puff pastry
all-purpose flour, for dusting
2 tbsp apricot jam
powdered sugar, for dusting
plant-based ice cream, to serve

- -

Preheat the oven Preheat the oven to 375°F (190°C). Line a baking sheet with parchment paper.

Squeeze the apples Place the grated apples in a clean kitchen towel or piece of muslin. Gather together the corners and twist to squeeze out excess moisture.

Mix In a large bowl, toss the grated apples with the cinnamon and semolina—the semolina helps absorb any remaining moisture.

Assemble Unroll the puff pastry sheet on a lightly floured surface and smooth out any creases. Spread the apricot jam evenly over the pastry, leaving a 1in (2.5cm) border around the edges. Evenly spread the cinnamon-coated grated apples over the jam-covered pastry, then carefully roll up the puff pastry from one end to the other, sealing the edges and ends to prevent the filling from spilling out.

Bake Transfer the strudel to the prepared baking sheet, seam-side down. Bake for 30–35 minutes, or until the puff pastry is golden brown and crisp.

Cool, dust, slice, and serve Allow the strudel to cool slightly on a wire rack. Just before serving, dust the top with powdered sugar for a touch of sweetness and elegance, then slice the strudel into pieces and serve warm. Add a scoop of plant-based vanilla ice cream on the side for an extra treat.

Storage Store leftovers in an airtight container at room temperature for up to 2 days. For longer storage, keep in the refrigerator for up to a week. Reheat in the oven before serving to restore crispness.

Fruit Leather

Remember those fruit roll-ups you loved as a kid? Well, I've been whipping up the homemade version, fruit leather! It's just as delicious but much healthier. It's the perfect way to use up any fruit that's about to go bad or is just overripe, and the best part? You know exactly what's in it: just fruit, a touch of sweetness, and nothing else.

Makes 3–5

Prep time 15 minutes

Cooking time 4–6 hours (drying time)

Ingredients

1lb 2oz (500g) assorted fruits (use ripe or surplus fruits)

2 tbsp chia seeds

1 tbsp maple or agave syrup

Blend Add all the ingredients to a blender and blend.

Pour and spread Line a large baking sheet with a silicone mat. Pour the blended mixture on to the prepared sheet and spread it out evenly with a spatula to form a thin layer.

Preheat the oven Preheat the oven to 175°F (100°C).

Dry Place the baking sheet in the oven and let dry out for 4–6 hours, checking periodically to see if it has reached the desired consistency.

Cut, roll, and store Cut the dried fruit sheet into thin strips. Roll up each strip and store in jars or airtight containers in a cool, dry place for up to 1 week.

Blend

Pour and spread

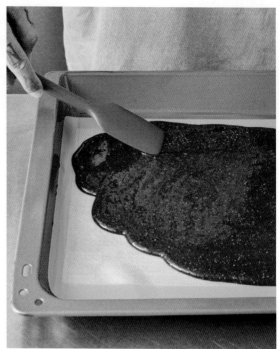

Dry

Cut and roll

Pineapple Chutney

By combining sweet and spicy, you will get a zingy chutney! Pineapple is incredibly versatile in the kitchen, and every single part can be used for something. The fruit is obviously great to enjoy as is, but if you want to bring it to the next level, you can preserve it and elevate its flavor by making a chutney, which will soon become your go-to for any burger filling or quick on-the-go sandwich.

Makes 2–2½ cups (500–600ml)

Prep time 15 minutes

Cooking time 45–60 minutes

Ingredients

4 tbsp coconut or olive oil

2 onions, finely chopped

4 garlic cloves, minced

2 tbsp freshly grated ginger

1 tsp mustard seeds

1 dried red chile, or to taste

1 tsp ground turmeric

1 tsp salt, or to taste

1 large pineapple, peeled, cored, and chopped into ¾in (1cm) chunks

2 oranges, peeled and diced into ¾in (1cm) chunks

½ cup (120ml) apple cider vinegar

6½ tbsp (80g) soft light brown sugar

Equipment

sterilized jars

Prepare the chutney Heat the oil in a large saucepan or pot over medium heat. Add the onions and garlic, and cook for 5-7 minutes until the onions are softened and translucent. Stir in the ginger, mustard seeds, dried red chili, turmeric, and salt, and cook for another 1-2 minutes until the spices are fragrant.

Add the pineapple and oranges, followed by the apple cider vinegar, and stir to combine. Finally, stir in the brown sugar and cook, stirring occasionally, until the sugar dissolves.

Simmer Bring the mixture to a boil, then reduce the heat to low. Simmer, uncovered, stirring occasionally, for 45-60 minutes. The chutney should thicken and the fruits should break down, creating a chunky sauce.

Taste and adjust Taste the chutney and adjust the seasoning if needed. You can add more salt, sugar, or vinegar to balance the flavors to your liking.

Cool Allow the chutney to cool to room temperature, then decant it into sterilized jars. It is now ready to serve or store.

Serve Serve the pineapple chutney as a tangy and sweet accompaniment to dishes like curries or grilled vegetables, or as a topping for sandwiches and burgers.

Storage Store in an airtight container in the refrigerator for to 2-3 weeks. You can freeze the chutney for up to 3 months. Thaw in the refrigerator before using.

Pineapple Tepache

Pineapple tepache is a refreshing and tangy fermented beverage that's perfect for hot days. Originating from Mexico, this drink is made by fermenting pineapple peels with sugar and spices, resulting in a sweet and fizzy delight. This is a great way to use up all your pineapple scraps, and the resulting drink is packed with probiotics and beneficial bacteria. I tried it for the first time at my friend's restaurant, Silo (a zero-waste restaurant in London), and I can't stop making it.

Makes 1 quart (1 liter)

Prep time 10 minutes

Fermentation time 2 days

Ingredients

peel of 1 pineapple

1 cup (200g) soft light brown sugar, plus extra to taste

1 cinnamon stick

4 cloves

4½ cups (1 liter) water

To serve

ice

pineapple chunks

mint leaves

Prepare the pineapple peel Rinse the pineapple peel thoroughly to remove any dirt or debris. Cut away any brown or woody parts.

Mix In a large glass jar or container, combine the pineapple peel with the brown sugar, cinnamon stick, cloves, and water. Stir well until the sugar has dissolved.

Ferment Cover the jar loosely with a clean cloth or kitchen towel. Place it in a warm, dark place to ferment for 2 days. Stir the mixture once or twice a day. After 2 days, check the tepache for signs of fermentation. It should be bubbly and have a slightly tangy aroma.

Strain Strain the fermented mixture through a fine mesh sieve or piece of muslin into a bowl or pitcher to remove the pineapple peels and spices. Press down on the solids to extract as much liquid as possible.

Taste and sweeten (optional) Taste the strained tepache and add additional sugar if desired, stirring until dissolved. Transfer to the refrigerator to chill.

Serve Pour the chilled tepache into serving glasses over ice. Garnish with pineapple chunks and fresh mint leaves, if desired, then serve.

Storage Store any leftover tepache in a sealed container in the refrigerator for up to 1 week. Shake well before serving, as it may settle during storage.

Dehydrated Strawberries

Imagine having the sweet taste of summer strawberries at your fingertips, any time of the year. That's exactly what you get with these dehydrated strawberries. This DIY snack is not just delicious; it's also a wholesome, no-waste way to enjoy your favorite fruit. Dehydrating strawberries concentrates their flavor, making them an irresistible snack and a perfect topping for cereals and yogurt. Plus, if you grind them into a fine powder, you have a secret ingredient for your baking adventures that will add a vibrant natural color and flavor that's nothing short of amazing. You can scale the quantities up or down depending on how much you want to make.

Makes 16–20 portions
Prep time 15 minutes
Dehydration time 6–12 hours

Ingredients
2¼lb (1kg) strawberries
2 tbsp lemon juice (optional)

Equipment
dehydrator

Prepare the strawberries Wash and hull the strawberries. Slice them uniformly for even dehydration. If desired, you can pretreat the sliced strawberries by dipping them in a bowl containing a mixture of lemon juice and water to preserve color and add a hint of tartness.

Dehydrate Arrange the sliced strawberries on the dehydrator trays, ensuring they don't overlap. Set the dehydrator temperature to 135°F (57°C) for optimal drying (adjust based on your dehydrator model). Dehydrate the strawberries for 6–12 hours, checking periodically to see if they are done. They are ready when they are firm, not sticky, and have a leathery texture. Now you can use them as they are for your granolas or baking, or you can transform them into powder (see below).

Cool and store Allow the dehydrated slices to cool completely before transferring to an airtight container or vacuum-sealed bags. Keep in a cool, dark place for 2–3 months.

Making strawberry powder
» To make a powder, place the dehydrated slices in a blender or food processor and blend until you achieve a fine powder. It should be dry, free-flowing, and clump-free. Store in an airtight container in a cool, dark place for 2–3 months.

Strawberry Cheong

This traditional Korean syrup is always popular during our little garden parties in the summer. It's sweet, tangy, and incredibly versatile. Whether you're mixing it into cocktails, adding a splash to sparkling water, or drizzling it over pancakes, it's a delightful way to bring a burst of strawberry flavor to your dishes. It's like drinking summer with every sip and is a great way to preserve strawberries at the peak of their flavor

Makes 1 quart (1 liter)

Prep time 15 minutes

Fermentation time 1 week

Ingredients

14oz (400g) strawberries, diced

2 lemons, diced (including the peels)

2 cups (400g) unrefined sugar

Equipment

1¾ pint (1 liter) sterilized jar

1¾ pint (1 liter) sterilized glass bottle

- -

Prepare the mixture In a large bowl, combine the diced strawberries and lemons with half of the sugar and stir.

Fill the jar Transfer the mixture into your jar, pressing it to the bottom. Top off the jar with the remaining sugar.

Ferment Cover the jar with a lid and leave in the fridge for up to a week until almost all the fruits have turned into syrup.

Strain Once it's ready, strain the syrup through a fine mesh sieve to remove the fruit solids. (This fruit pulp can be added to an ice-cube tray, topped off with water, and frozen to create flavored ice cubes.)

Store Pour the strained cheong syrup into the sterilized bottle. It will keep in the fridge for up to a month.

~~~~~~~~~~

Strawberry cheong drink

» To create a refreshing drink, add 1 tablespoon of cheong to a pint glass. Add some fruity ice cubes, and top off with sparkling water or lemonade.

Preserved Lemon Peel

I've been on a low-waste mission for many years, and let me tell you, preserving lemon peels has opened up a whole new world of flavor. It's like capturing the essence of sunshine in a jar: zesty, tangy, and incredibly versatile. Use these preserved peels in sandwiches and salads, blend into a paste for vinaigrette, or get creative with your culinary inventions.

Makes 1lb 2oz (500g)
Prep time 10 minutes
Cooking time 20 minutes

Ingredients
skins of 6–8 squeezed
   lemons
4 tbsp salt
6 tbsp olive oil
2 garlic cloves
1–3 tbsp herbs or other
   spices (I like to use a mix of
   lemon thyme, oregano,
   and chives, but experiment
   to find the flavors you like
   best)

- -

Prepare the peels Dice the lemon peels into small cubes.

Boil Place the lemon peels in a large saucepan and fill with water. Bring to a boil and boil for 20 minutes or until the peels are tender. Drain, reserving the water in a bowl—you can use this to make iced tea or lemonade (see right). Let the cooked lemon peels cool.

Mix Once the peels are cooled, mix with the salt, olive oil, garlic, and your chosen herbs.

Store Store the mixture in an airtight container in the fridge for up to 2 weeks. They're ready to use immediately, but the flavor will intensify with time.

Purple Lemonade

Using the leftover water from boiling the peels (see left), we're going to craft a drink that's not just refreshing but also a feast for the eyes. When infused in hot water, pea flowers release a beautiful blue color. When you add lemon, its acidity turns the liquid purple or pink. Magic!

Serves 4–6
Prep time 5 minutes
Cooking time 10 minutes

Ingredients
4¼ cups (1 liter) leftover
   water from boiling
   lemon peels (see left)
1 cup dried butterfly pea
   flowers
1 cup (200g) superfine
   sugar, or to taste

To serve
ice cubes
lemon slices
mint leaves
club soda (optional)

- -

Make the lemonade Bring the lemon water to a boil in a large saucepan. Add the butterfly pea flowers, then take the pan off the heat and let infuse for 5–7 minutes. Strain to remove the flowers. Add the sugar, adjusting the quantity to taste.

Chill Pour into a pitcher and chill for at least 2 hours.

Serve Pour the purple lemonade over ice cubes in glasses. Garnish with lemon slices and fresh mint leaves for an extra layer of flavor. If you like, you can top it off with club soda.

Storage Store any leftovers in a covered container in the refrigerator. Consume within 1–2 days.

Candied Chocolate Orange Peel

Transforming orange peels into candied chocolate orange peel has been an obsession of mine since I was a kid. (Actually, perhaps the obsession was more about eating them than making them, haha!) I remember I couldn't wait to finish dinner in order to eat this luxurious treat, that feels like one of those fancy chocolates you see in boutiques. The process of candying peel might sound complicated, but it's surprisingly simple and so rewarding. Not only is it a fantastic way to reduce waste, but it also results in a decadent snack or a sophisticated gift for your foodie friends. It's all about turning the overlooked into the irresistible.

Makes about 48 pieces

Prep time 20 minutes

Cooking time 5 minutes, plus drying time

Ingredients

peels of 3 oranges, sliced to your
   preferred size
5¾oz (160g) dark chocolate (at
   least 70 percent cocoa solids),
   broken into pieces
½ cup (80g) chopped almonds
flaky sea salt (optional)

Prepare the orange peels Blanch the peels by submerging them in boiling water for 1–2 minutes. Drain and repeat the process once more. This will reduce bitterness. Place the blanched peels on a wire rack to cool and dry—this will take about 20–30 minutes.

Make the chocolate coating Melt the chocolate in a heatproof bowl set over a pan of barely simmering water. Once melted, stir in the chopped almonds.

Coat and cool Dip the dried orange peels in the chocolate mixture to coat, then place them on a baking sheet lined with parchment paper, sprinkle with sea salt (if using) and let cool.

Storage Store the candied chocolate orange peels in an airtight container. They will last around 2 months.

Whole Orange Almond Cake

Did you know that you could use a whole orange to bake a delicious cake? The result is moist and fragrant, with a depth of flavor that's hard to beat. This cake is a celebration of simplicity and sustainability, using the entire orange to minimize waste. We quite often enjoy it for breakfast. The combination of citrusy sweetness with the nuttiness of almonds creates a texture and taste that's absolutely divine.

Serves 8–10

Prep time 15 minutes

Cooking time 35–40 minutes

Ingredients

1 whole orange

2½ cups (250g) almond flour

¾ cup (150g) granulated sugar

⅔ cup (85g) potato starch, plus extra if needed

4 tsp baking powder

5 tbsp water

- -

Preheat the oven Preheat the oven to 375°F (190°C) and line a 9in (24cm) round cake pan with parchment paper.

Mix the batter Add all the ingredients to a food processor, along with the water. Blend until it forms a thick paste. If the mixture is too runny, you can add another 1 tablespoon of potato starch.

Bake Transfer the mixture to the prepared pan. Bake for 35–40 minutes. Test for doneness by inserting a skewer into the middle of the cake; if it comes out clean, the cake is ready. Remove from the oven and let cool in the pan for a few minutes, then transfer to a wire rack to cool completely.

Storage This cake will keep in an airtight container in the refrigerator for 4 days.

Găluște cu Prune (Plum Dumplings)

A taste of Romanian tradition and Iasmina's favorite dessert. Have you ever tried sweet dumplings? It's time to give it a go. These soft potato dumplings filled with juicy plums and dusted with cinnamon sugar are the essence of late summer, and the perfect way to use seasonal ingredients, elevating their flavor.

Serves 4–6

Prep time 30 minutes

Cooking time 5–10 minutes

Ingredients

2 cups mashed potatoes, cooled

3–4 tbsp all-purpose flour

1 tbsp bread crumbs

10–20 plums (depending on size), pitted

For the coating

3 tbsp plant-based butter or vegetable oil

½ cup bread crumbs

1 tbsp ground cinnamon

2 tbsp soft brown sugar

2 tbsp ground almonds

Prepare the dumpling dough In a large bowl, mix the cooled mashed potatoes with the flour and bread crumbs until a soft but workable dough is formed. Add more flour if necessary to achieve a dough that can be shaped without sticking too much.

Form the dumplings Divide the dough into small portions, each one large enough to wrap around a plum. Flatten each portion slightly and place a pitted plum in the center. Carefully wrap the dough around the plum, pinching the edges to seal it completely. Repeat with the remaining dough and plums.

Cook the dumplings Bring a large pot of lightly salted water to a boil. Gently drop the dumplings into the boiling water, working in batches if necessary to avoid overcrowding. Cook for 5–10 minutes until the dumplings float to the surface and are cooked through. Use a slotted spoon to remove them from the water and set them aside while you cook the rest.

Prepare the coating Heat the plant-based butter or oil in a large skillet over medium heat. Add the bread crumbs and cook, stirring frequently, until the bread crumbs are golden brown and crispy. Pour the toasted bread crumbs into a bowl and add the cinnamon, brown sugar, and ground almonds. Stir to combine.

Coat the dumplings While the dumplings are still warm, gently roll them in the cinnamon-and-almond bread crumb mixture to coat evenly.

Serve Serve the plum dumplings warm as a dessert or a hearty snack. They can be enjoyed on their own or with a dollop of plant-based cream or yogurt if desired.

Storage Store leftover dumplings in an airtight container in the refrigerator for up to 3 days. Reheat gently in a pan or in a low oven before serving. The cooked dumplings can also be frozen for up to 2 months. Place them in a single layer on a baking sheet to freeze individually, then transfer to a freezer bag or container. Reheat thoroughly from frozen in the oven or a skillet.

Fig Leaf Panna Cotta

Did you know that you can eat fig leaves? When dried, they have a nutty, coconutty, earthy flavor. I learned about this during a foraging course in 2019, when the guide handed me a piece of dry leaf and said, "Try it!" I wasn't sure, but once I tried it, I couldn't believe how tasty it was.

Serves 4
Prep time 10 minutes
Cooking time 10 minutes, plus at least 4 hours to set

Ingredients

6 dried fig leaves
2 × 14oz (400g) cans coconut milk
3 tbsp superfine sugar
1 tbsp vanilla bean paste
1 tbsp ground agar agar

To serve
chopped mango or other fruit of your choice
shredded coconut

- -

Preheat the oven Preheat the oven to 400°F (200°C).

Prepare the fig leaves Place the dried fig leaves on a baking tray and bake for 5–7 minutes—this will enhance their flavor. Let cool.

Infuse the coconut milk Combine the coconut milk and sugar in a saucepan over medium heat. Warm through, stirring occasionally, until the sugar dissolves. Add the vanilla paste and dried fig leaves to the saucepan, and let it all simmer gently for 5 minutes to infuse the coconut milk with the fig-leaf flavor.

Prepare the agar agar In a small bowl, dissolve the agar agar in a small amount of water according to the packet instructions. Stir until fully dissolved.

Mix Once the coconut milk has been infused with the fig-leaf flavor, remove the fig leaves from the saucepan. Gradually pour the dissolved agar agar into the coconut milk mixture, stirring continuously. Mix well to ensure the agar agar is evenly distributed.

Set Divide the coconut milk mixture evenly among four panna cotta molds or ramekins. Let cool slightly at room temperature before transferring to the refrigerator for at least 4 hours, or until set and firm.

Serve Carefully unmold the set panna cotta onto serving plates. Serve with chopped mango or the fruit of your choice, sprinkled with shredded coconut.

Storage Store any leftover panna cotta in an airtight container in the refrigerator for up to 3 days.

Green Fig Syrup

These unripe figs in syrup are filled with intense flavor and make the perfect topping for any dessert.

Makes 4–5 × 8oz (250ml) jars
Prep time 20 minutes
Cooking time 45 minutes

Ingredients

2¼lb (1kg) green figs
3¾ cups (750g) granulated sugar
2 cups (475ml) water
1 vanilla pod
1 lemon, thinly sliced (seeds removed)
1 tbsp brandy or rum (optional)

Equipment
4 sterilized 8oz (250ml) jars

Prepare the figs Thoroughly wash the figs and remove any stems or blemishes. Cut a small cross at the base of each fig to allow the syrup to penetrate.

Make the syrup In a large saucepan, combine the granulated sugar with the water over medium heat. Cook, stirring, for about 2 minutes until the sugar dissolves completely. Split the vanilla pod lengthwise and scrape out the seeds using the back of a knife. Add them to the syrup and stir.

Add figs and simmer Carefully add the prepared green figs and the lemon slices to the simmering syrup. Reduce the heat to low and simmer gently for 30–40 minutes, or until the figs are tender but still hold their shape. Stir occasionally to ensure even cooking. If desired, add a tablespoon of brandy or rum to the syrup during the last 5 minutes of cooking for an extra flavor boost.

Cool Remove the pan from the heat and let cool for about 15 minutes.

Transfer to jars Carefully pack the figs and syrup into sterilized jars, ensuring that each jar has a good balance of figs and syrup. Seal the jars tightly.

Storage Store in a cool, dark place for up to 1 year. Once opened, refrigerate any remaining figs and consume within 1 month.

Stuffed Figs

Elevate the flavor of your figs with a few simple ingredients, combining sweet and savory for the perfect balance of pure delight.

Makes 12
Prep time 15 minutes

Ingredients

12 ripe figs
7oz (200g) Plant-Based Ricotta (see p164)
½ cup walnuts, finely chopped
2 tbsp balsamic vinegar

To serve (optional)
thyme leaves and maple syrup

Prepare the figs Rinse the figs under cold water and pat them dry with a paper towel. Using a sharp knife, cut a cross shape into the top of each fig, cutting about three-quarters of the way down, creating an opening for the stuffing.

Make the filling In a mixing bowl, combine the ricotta with the chopped walnuts. Mix well until evenly combined.

Stuff the figs Using a teaspoon, gently stuff each fig with the ricotta and walnut mixture, filling the cavity created by the crosscut. Press down gently to compact the filling.

Drizzle Drizzle the stuffed figs with the balsamic vinegar, ensuring each fig gets a light coating.

Serve Sprinkle fresh thyme leaves over the stuffed figs for added flavor and presentation. For extra sweetness, drizzle the stuffed figs with maple syrup just before serving, if desired. Arrange the figs on a serving platter and serve immediately as an appetizer or dessert.

Storage These stuffed figs are best enjoyed fresh and should be served soon after preparation. If storing leftovers, refrigerate in an airtight container for up to 1 day, but note that the texture may change slightly upon chilling.

Date Bites

Let me introduce you to date bites—your new favorite snack. These little gems are a powerhouse of nutrition and flavor, all packed into one delicious mouthful. They're like mini energy bombs.

Makes 20 bites
Prep time 20 minutes

Ingredients
20 medjool dates
20 whole almonds
7oz (200g) dark chocolate (at least 70 percent cocoa solids)
⅓ cup (40g) shelled pistachios, finely chopped

- - - - - - - - - - - - - - - -

Stuff the dates Make a small incision along the side of each date and remove the seeds (you can save them to make coffee; see right). Gently open each date and insert a whole almond.

Melt the chocolate Melt the chocolate in a heatproof bowl set over a pan of barely simmering water.

Coat Dip each date into the melted chocolate, ensuring it's well coated. While the chocolate is still wet, sprinkle with the pistachios.

Set and chill Place the chocolate-coated and pistachio-topped date bites on a baking sheet lined with parchment paper to set. Once cool, transfer the bites to the refrigerator for at least 10-15 minutes to allow the chocolate to harden. Once the chocolate is firm, remove the date bites from the refrigerator and serve.

Storage Store in an airtight container in the refrigerator for up to 1 week.

Date Seed Coffee

Who knew that the humble date seed could be the secret to your new favorite coffee alternative? Date seed coffee is an aromatic brew that's surprisingly coffeelike but without the caffeine kick.

Makes 14 servings
Prep time 15 minutes, plus drying time
Cooking time 20-30 minutes

Ingredients
40 dates with seeds (or 40 seeds, if you have them)

- - - - - - - - - - - - - - - -

Separate pulp and seeds If using whole dates, divide the pulp from the seeds. Keep the pulp to make your own date paste (simply blend the pulp in a blender until smooth), or store in an airtight container to use in another recipe.

Wash and dry the seeds Wash the date seeds, then spread them out on a baking sheet to air-dry for a few days. If you prefer, use a dehydrator at 130°F (54°C) for 24 hours.

Roast Preheat the oven to 350°F (180°C). Spread out the seeds on a baking sheet. Roast for 20-30 minutes until fragrant and lightly browned. Cool.

Grind Once cool, transfer the roasted seeds to a blender and grind into a fine powder. The resulting powder will have a coffeelike aroma.

Storage Keep the ground date seed powder in an airtight container at room temperature. It will keep for up to 3 months.

Brewing the coffee
» To make a cup of date seed coffee, mix ¾ teaspoon of the ground date seed powder with hot water and stir to dissolve. Enjoy.

Herbs

Mixed Herbs

Herb Salt   156
Herb Butter   156
Herb Bombs   156

Mixed Herbs

Fresh herbs are a cornerstone of flavorful cooking, and growing your own ensures you have a constant supply of aromatic ingredients. From basil to rosemary, each herb brings its unique flavor and health benefits to your dishes. You could even plant different variations of common herbs, like lemon thyme or pineapple sage. I always try to research the most unusual varieties to unlock new flavors in the kitchen, but I surely couldn't cook what I cook without an array of common herbs always growing, either indoors or outdoors.

Herb Salt

Sprinkle this over soups and salads for a hit of herbal flavor.

Makes about 7oz (200g)
Prep time 15 minutes
Cooking time 30–45 minutes (optional, for faster drying)

Ingredients
¼ cup (20g) mixed herbs (e.g., rosemary, thyme, sage, oregano)
¾ cup (200g) coarse salt or rock salt

- - - - - - - - - - - - - - - - -

Mix Add the herbs to a blender and blend to combine. Add the salt and pulse until fully incorporated.

Dry Spread out the mixture in an even layer on a baking sheet and let dry in a well-ventilated spot. To speed up the process, you can place the sheet in an oven heated to 230°F (130°C) for 30–45 minutes, keeping an eye on it so it doesn't burn.

Storage Store in an airtight container at room temperature. The herb salt will keep for several months.

Herb Butter

Spread on bread or stir into soups and sauces.

Makes 9oz (250g)
Prep time 15 minutes

Ingredients
2 tbsp (10g) fresh herbs (e.g., chives, parsley, dill, or tarragon), roughly chopped
1 tsp lemon zest
9oz (250g) plant-based butter
salt (optional)

- - - - - - - - - - - - - - - - -

Mix In a bowl, mix the chopped herbs with the lemon zest and butter until fully incorporated. Taste and season with salt if desired.

Shape and chill Place the herb butter mixture on a piece of biodegradable plastic wrap, and roll tightly to form a log. Chill until firm.

Storage Store the herb butter in the refrigerator for up to 2 weeks. For longer storage, you can freeze it for up to 3 months.

Herb Bomb

Kick-start a stir-fry or a quick dinner.

Makes about 12
Prep time 10 minutes

Ingredients
¼ cup (20g) mixed herbs (e.g., basil, parsley, cilantro, rosemary, or thyme), roughly chopped
2–3 garlic cloves, minced (optional)
1 cup (240ml) extra-virgin olive oil

- - - - - - - - - - - - - - - - -

Prepare the herb bombs Spoon about 1 teaspoon of herbs into each mold in an ice-cube tray. Divide the garlic between them if using, then pour over the olive oil, leaving a tiny gap at the top of each mold to prevent overflow.

Freeze Place in the freezer until completely frozen.

Storage Once frozen, remove the herb bombs and transfer them to a freezer-safe bag or container. They will keep for several months in the freezer.

Herb
Salt

Herb
Butter

Herb
Bombs

Flour-Based Recipes

Pasta	Vegetable Pasta Dough	**162**
	Plant-Based Ricotta	**164**
	Simple Pasta Sauce	**164**
Focaccia	Beet Focaccia	**165**
Quiche	Zucchini Quiche	**169**
Sourdough	Sourdough Starter	**170**
	Sourdough Bread	**172**
	Sourdough Discard Crackers	**173**
Cereal	Cocoa Peanut Butter Cereal	**174**

Vegetable Pasta Dough

This a tribute to my Italian origins: homemade pasta made to a sort of untraditional recipe, but using fresh produce from my garden. It reminds me of spending Sundays at my grandparents' house, helping my grandma make fresh pasta and picking vegetables from my grandpa's garden.

Serves 2–4

Prep time 15 minutes, plus resting time

Cooking time 1–2 minutes

Ingredients

2¾ cups (340g) "00" flour, plus extra for dusting

1 tsp salt

6oz (170g) vegetables of your choice, puréed or very finely chopped

7 tbsp aquafaba (the liquid from canned chickpeas)

Optional

Plant-Based Ricotta (see p164)

Simple Pasta Sauce (see p164)

- -

Mix the dough Combine the flour, salt, and puréed vegetables in a large bowl. Gradually add the aquafaba and knead to form a smooth dough.

Rest Wrap the dough in biodegradable plastic wrap and let rest in the fridge for 30 minutes.

Shape the pasta Roll out the dough on a floured surface to a thickness of ⅛in (2–3mm) and cut it into your desired shapes. If you're making ravioli, cut it into circles or squares and fill each one with a small spoonful of my Plant-Based Ricotta (see p164), using extra aquafaba to seal the edges.

Cook the pasta Bring a large pan of salted water to a boil. Add the pasta and cook for 1–2 minutes, or until al dente. Drain and serve. This pasta is perfect paired with my Simple Pasta Sauce (see p164).

Storage Raw pasta dough can be stored in the fridge for up to 2 days. Cooked pasta should be consumed immediately for best quality.

Plant-Based Ricotta

Ricotta was always a staple food at my grandma's house. As a quick dessert or an afternoon treat, she used to whip up ricotta, sugar, and lemon—and let me tell you, that was a dream snack. When I decided to adopt a plant-based diet, I didn't want to give up on certain flavors, so I tried to find the best alternatives. You can make your cashew ricotta salty or sweet—here, I've shared a savory version with herbs and garlic. It's delicious simply spread on bread but also makes the creamiest filling for your ravioli.

Makes about 1–2 cups (240–475ml)
Prep time 10 minutes, plus soaking

Ingredients
2 cups (300g) cashews
½ tsp finely chopped sage
½ tsp finely chopped chives
½ tsp finely chopped parsley
1 garlic clove, minced (optional)
½ cup (120ml) water
salt and freshly ground black pepper

- - - - - - - - - - - - - - - - - -

Soak the cashews Place the cashews in a large bowl and pour over enough water to cover them by about 1in (2.5cm). Let soak for 3 hours.

Make the ricotta Drain the soaked cashews and pour them into a blender. Add the herbs and garlic (if using). Pour in the ½ cup of water, and blend to achieve a ricotta-like consistency, adding more water if needed. Season to taste with salt and pepper.

Storage Store in an airtight container in the refrigerator for 3–4 days.

Simple Pasta Sauce

Pair this simple sauce with my homemade pasta on page 162.

Makes enough sauce for 2–4 servings of pasta
Prep time 10 minutes
Cooking time 20–30 minutes

Ingredients
4 tbsp olive oil
1 onion, chopped
1 garlic clove, minced
1 celery stick, chopped
1 tsp chopped sage
9–14oz (250–400g) mixed tomatoes, chopped
salt and freshly ground black pepper

- - - - - - - - - - - - - - - - - -

Make the sauce Heat the olive oil in a saucepan over medium heat. Add the onion, garlic, and celery, and sauté for 5–10 minutes until softened. Season to taste with salt and pepper, then stir in the sage and chopped tomatoes. Reduce the heat to low and simmer for 15–20 minutes until the sauce thickens.

Serve Serve with your pasta.

Storage Store any leftover sauce in the refrigerator for 3–4 days.

Beet Focaccia

Focaccia is a staple food in Italy, and we make it almost once a week at home because it's extremely easy and the perfect appetizer when people come over. As much as we love the plain version, adding beets brings a whole new level of color and flavor. This beet focaccia looks incredible and is great as an accompaniment to meals or as a delicious snack on its own.

Serves 8–10

Prep time 20 minutes, plus proofing

Cooking time 25–30 minutes

Ingredients

1 tsp superfine sugar

1¾ cup (400ml) warm water

¼oz (7g) instant yeast (1 packet)

3¼ cups (400g) bread flour

2–3 tbsp beet powder (see Vegetable Skin Powders, p34)

2 tsp salt

6 tbsp olive oil, plus extra for oiling

For the topping

4 tbsp olive oil

6 tbsp beet juice

10 garlic cloves, thinly sliced

1 tbsp finely chopped rosemary needles

Activate the yeast In a small bowl, combine the sugar with the warm water. Sprinkle the instant yeast over the water and let it sit for about 5 minutes until frothy.

Mix the dough In a mixing bowl, whisk together the bread flour, beet powder, and salt. Make a well in the center and pour in the activated yeast mixture and olive oil. Mix until a dough begins to form. Knead for 2–3 minutes to combine, being careful not to overknead. The dough will look a bit rough, but this will improve with proofing.

First proof and fold Cover the bowl with biodegradable plastic wrap and let rest for 30 minutes. After 30 minutes, with oiled hands, fold the outer four corners of the dough toward the center. This helps strengthen the dough structure.

Second proof and fold Cover the bowl and let rise for another 30 minutes, then repeat the folding process above.

Overnight proof Cover once more and refrigerate overnight, or for 8–10 hours.

Shape and final proof Grease a baking sheet with olive oil. Remove the dough from the refrigerator and gently stretch and shape it into a rectangular shape to fit the baking sheet. Cover with biodegradable plastic wrap and let rise for about 1 hour, or until doubled in size.

Preheat the oven Preheat the oven to 475°F (240°C).

Top and bake Once the dough has doubled in size, drizzle the 4 tablespoons of olive oil for the topping over the surface. Use your fingers to create dimples all over the dough; this will help the bubbles form and create a lovely texture. Drizzle the beet juice over the dough, then sprinkle the sliced garlic cloves and fresh rosemary on top. Bake for 25–30 minutes, or until the focaccia is golden and cooked through.

Cool and serve Remove from the baking sheet and cool on a wire rack for at least 10 minutes, then slice. Enjoy warm or at room temperature.

Storage Store leftover focaccia in an airtight container at room temperature for up to 3 days, or refrigerate for up to 1 week. Reheat in the oven to restore crispness. The focaccia can also be frozen for up to 2 months.

Knead and proof

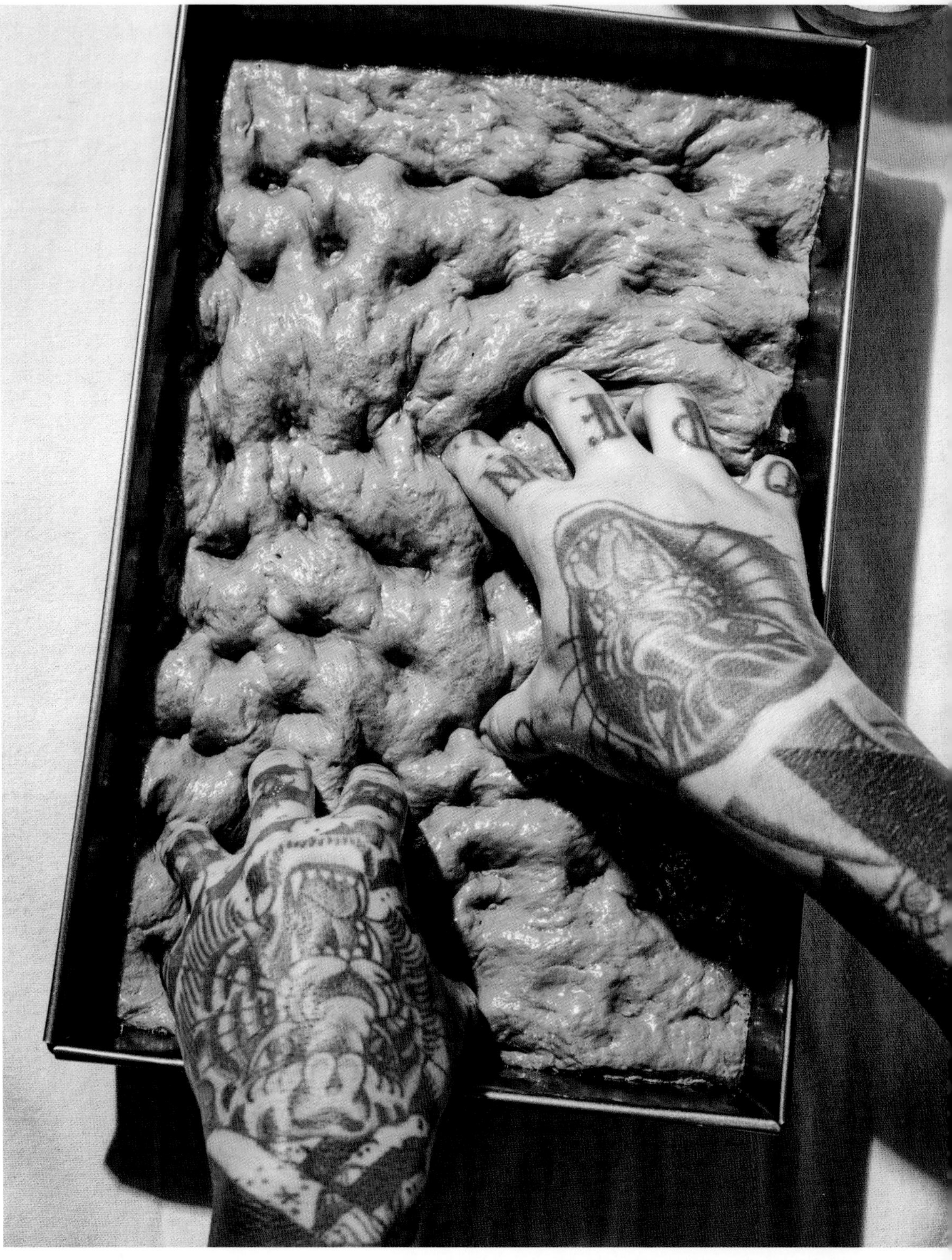

Decorate

Cool

Zucchini Quiche

When I think about summer, there are many crops that come to mind, but zucchini are definitely among them. This flaky, crunchy dish encapsulates the essence of summer in every bite!

Serves 6–8

Prep time 30 minutes

Cooking time 50 minutes

Ingredients

For the pastry

1 tbsp ground flaxseed

1 cup plus 2 tbsp (150g) whole wheat flour, plus extra for dusting

¾ cup (70g) ground almonds

5 tbsp chilled plant-based butter, diced

For the filling

2 tbsp olive oil

1 onion, finely chopped

2 zucchini

1lb (450g) firm tofu, drained

½ cup (120ml) soy milk

4 tsp cornstarch or potato starch

2 tbsp nutritional yeast

¼ tsp ground turmeric

2–3 garlic cloves, minced

1 tsp mustard (not whole grain)

pinch of salt

¼ tsp freshly ground black pepper

Make a flax egg In a small bowl, mix the ground flaxseed with 3 tablespoons water. Stir well, then let sit for about 5 minutes to thicken.

Make the pastry dough In a large bowl, combine the flour and ground almonds. Add the chilled plant-based butter and use your fingers to work it into the flour until the mixture resembles coarse crumbs. Stir in the flax egg and mix until the dough starts to come together. If the dough is too dry, add a small amount of cold water, a tablespoon at a time.

Chill Form the dough into a disc, wrap it in biodegradable plastic wrap, and refrigerate for at least 30 minutes.

Preheat the oven Preheat the oven to 400°F (200°C).

Sauté the vegetables Heat the olive oil in a skillet over medium heat. Add the onion and cook for 5 minutes until softened, then slice one of the zucchini and add to the pan. Cook for 3–5 minutes until tender. Set aside to cool.

Prepare the tofu mixture Add the drained tofu to a food processor, along with the soy milk, cornstarch or potato starch, nutritional yeast, turmeric, garlic, mustard, salt, and pepper. Blend until smooth and creamy.

Make the pastry crust On a lightly floured surface, roll out the chilled dough until it's big enough to line a 9in (23cm) tart pan or pie dish. Transfer to the pan or dish and press it evenly into the bottom and sides. Bake for 10 minutes, then remove from the oven and let cool slightly.

Add the filling Pour the tofu mixture into the prebaked crust, spreading it out evenly. Top with the sautéed zucchini and onion mixture.

Decorate Slice the remaining zucchini into thin half-moons. Arrange these on top of the quiche in an overlapping, fish-scale pattern.

Bake Bake for 35–40 minutes until the filling is set and the top is slightly golden.

Cool and serve Let the quiche cool for at least 10 minutes before slicing. This helps the filling set and makes it easier to cut clean slices. Serve warm or at room temperature. The quiche is great on its own or with a fresh salad.

Storage Store in an airtight container in the refrigerator for up to 4 days. It can also be frozen for up to 2 months. Thaw in the refrigerator overnight and reheat in the oven before serving.

Sourdough Starter

I decided to dive into the world of wild yeast, and guess what? Creating my own sourdough starter was like unlocking a secret baking superpower. It's a bit like having a pet you can eat ... uh, in a nonweird way. Every day, you feed it and watch it grow, and it rewards you with the most amazing bread. There's something magical about baking with something that's alive, that you've nurtured. Plus, it's a gateway to not just bread but also pancakes, waffles, and so much more.

Makes 1 starter

Prep time 10 minutes (spread over 7 days

Ingredients

1 cup (140g) bread flour

1 cup (240ml) water

For each feeding

1 cup (140g) bread flour

1 cup (240ml) water

Day 1: Begin the journey Combine the flour with the water in a jar. Mix well with a fork and cover loosely with a piece of muslin secured with an elastic band or string, then place in a warm spot.

Day 2: Patience is a virtue Nothing to do but wait. If "hooch" (dark liquid) appears on top of your starter, pour it off and discard.

Day 3: Discard and feed Remove half of your starter from the jar and "discard." Of course, we don't actually discard it. You can use the discarded portion to make delicious crackers (see p173) or similar recipes. "Feed" your starter with another 1 cup of flour and 1 cup of water.

Days 4, 5, and 6: Repeat and reuse Keep repeating the discard-and-feed process.

Day 7: Bubbling with excitement Your starter should be ready, with plenty of bubbles. Turn to page 172 to find out how to make your own sourdough bread.

Storage Keep your sourdough starter in the refrigerator when not in use. If you get into a regular baking pattern, you may find that you don't need to refrigerate it as you'll be constantly feeding and using it. If you do keep the starter in the refrigerator for a while, you'll need to "feed" it for about a week before it's ready to use again.

Sourdough Bread

I've never been great at baking, but after my adventure into the world of sourdough starters, I was itching to bake my first loaf. And let me tell you, there's nothing quite like pulling your own sourdough bread out of the oven. The smell, the crackle of the crust, the warm, airy interior—it's pure magic. This isn't just bread; it's a labor of love that's surprisingly simple but incredibly rewarding.

Makes 1 loaf

Prep time 15 minutes, plus proofing time

Cooking time 1 hour

Ingredients

4 cups (500g) bread flour

1 tsp salt

1½ cups (360ml) lukewarm water

⅔ cup (120g) Sourdough Starter (see p170)

Mix and knead In a large bowl, combine the flour and salt with the lukewarm water. Knead until the mixture is uniform and elastic. Add the starter to the mixture and combine slowly to evenly integrate.

Proof Cover the bowl with a clean kitchen towel and let the dough rise for 5–12 hours, depending on the room temperature, until it doubles in size.

Shape and rest Transfer the dough to a baking sheet lined with parchment paper. Shape it into a round ball and let rest for 30 minutes.

Preheat and bake Preheat the oven to 475°F (240°C). Preheat a baking container such as a casserole dish with a lid for 10 minutes, then place the dough inside the preheated container. Spray the cover with water for humidity. Bake for 30 minutes with the cover on, then remove the cover and bake for another 30 minutes until the bread is golden brown.

Rest and serve Allow the freshly baked bread to rest for 20 minutes before slicing and serving.

Storage The bread will keep in an airtight container for up to a week. Alternatively, you can freeze the bread for longer storage.

Using up stale bread: Croutons and bread crumbs

» To make delicious croutons, cut stale bread into bite-sized cubes, drizzle with olive oil, and sprinkle over some dried herbs (such as oregano, parsley, or thyme) and a little garlic powder. Season with salt and pepper and bake at 400°F (200°C) for 15 minutes until crunchy.

» To make crunchy golden bread crumbs, break stale bread into 1in (2.5cm) pieces and bake at 400°F (200°C) for 10–15 minutes until dry and crisp. Let cool completely, then pulse in a food processor. Store the bread crumbs in an airtight container in a cool, dry place, and use within a month for optimal freshness.

Sourdough Discard Crackers

When you "feed" your sourdough starter (see p170), use the discarded starter to make these delicious crackers.

Makes 2 trays of crackers

Prep time 15 minutes, plus chilling

Cook time 25 minutes

Ingredients

1 cup (225g) Sourdough Starter, unfed or discarded (see p170)

1 cup (115g) whole wheat flour, plus extra for dusting

½ tsp fine sea salt

4 tbsp unsalted plant-based butter, at room temperature

2 tbsp dried herbs of your choice (optional)

olive oil, for brushing

coarse salt (such as kosher or sea salt), for sprinkling

- -

Mix the dough In a mixing bowl, combine the sourdough starter, flour, fine sea salt, butter, and dried herbs. Mix until the dough comes together into a smooth, nonsticky ball.

Chill Divide the dough into two even portions. Flatten each portion into a rectangular shape. Wrap them in biodegradable plastic wrap and place them in the refrigerator for at least 30 minutes, or until firm.

Preheat the oven Preheat your oven to 350°F (180°C) and line two baking sheets with parchment paper.

Roll out the dough and cut Take one portion of dough out of the fridge. On a lightly floured surface, roll it out using a rolling pin until it's very thin—about ¹⁄₁₆in (1.5mm) thick. Don't worry if the edges are rough. Carefully transfer the rolled-out dough to one of the prepared baking sheets. Brush the top with a light coating of olive oil and sprinkle with coarse salt. Use a sharp knife or a pizza cutter to slice the dough into small squares, about 1in (2.5cm) across.

Use a fork to prick each cracker a couple of times to prevent them from puffing up, then repeat the rolling and cutting process with the second portion of dough.

Bake Bake the crackers for 20–25 minutes, or until the edges are just starting to turn golden brown, rotating the baking sheets halfway through for even baking.

Cool Let the crackers cool completely on a wire rack before serving.

Storage Store in an airtight container at room temperature for about a week.

Cocoa Peanut Butter Cereal

Did you ever wonder how to kick-start your morning with something delicious and yet super simple to make? This cereal is like your childhood favorite but reimagined with a wholesome twist—it's free from chemicals and ideal for kids. Homemade cereals are my little nod to enjoying the simple pleasures in life, all while keeping things nutritious.

Serves 4

Prep time 15 minutes

Cooking time 12 minutes

Ingredients

2 cups (270g) all-purpose flour

½ cup (65g) coconut flour

½ tsp baking soda

½ tsp baking powder

½ cup (100g) cane sugar or coconut sugar

1 tbsp oil (such as sesame seed, olive, or coconut)

1 cup (240ml) almond milk, plus extra if needed

6 tbsp cocoa powder

½ tsp ground cinnamon

4 tbsp smooth peanut butter

Equipment

piping bag (optional)

Mix the batter In a large bowl, mix together the flour, coconut flour, baking soda, baking powder, and sugar. Give it a good stir, then add the oil and almond milk. Combine until you have a smooth, sticky batter.

Divide and flavor Divide the batter between 2 bowls. To one, add the cocoa powder. To the other, add the cinnamon and peanut butter. Stir well. Both mixtures should be soft enough to shape using a piping bag or your hands. If this isn't the case, add another splash of almond milk.

Preheat the oven Preheat the oven to 400°F (200°C).

Shape the spheres Using your hands or a piping bag, shape both mixtures into small spheres (maximum ½in/1cm in diameter), placing them on a baking sheet. Remember they will rise slightly while baking. If you decide to make larger spheres, you'll need to adjust the baking time accordingly.

Bake Bake for 12 minutes. Let cool completely on the baking sheet.

Store The cereal will keep in an airtight container in a cool, dry place for up to 1 month.

Home
Remedies

Skin Salve   Lavender Skin Salve   178

Hand Soap   Chocolate and Coffee   180
                Calendula and Lemon   180
                Lavender and Oats   180
                Orange and Rosemary   180

Lip Balm   Mint Lip Balm   183

Shower Steamers   Eucalyptus Shower Steamers   184

Lavender Skin Salve

We normally hang lavender around the house to dry, and it makes our entire home smell like spring. Once dried, we use the lavender to create this incredible skin salve, which helps with a range of issues. Lavender has natural anti-inflammatory and soothing properties, which can help reduce irritation on the skin and promote better sleep. It also possesses antibacterial qualities, making it useful in treating acne. Its regenerative properties can aid in the healing of cuts, burns, and other minor skin injuries. Lavender can also be used in moisturizing products to hydrate the skin without making it oily.

Makes about 1 cup (250ml)

Prep time 5–7 days for drying the lavender, 30 days for oil infusion

Cooking time 5 minutes

Ingredients

3–5 bunches of fresh lavender

1 cup (240ml) cold-pressed sunflower oil

3 tbsp soy wax or beeswax

Equipment

small tubs or containers

Dry the lavender Hang the fresh lavender upside down to dry at room temperature for 5–7 days.

Infuse the oil Once the lavender is dry, remove the stems and separate out the lavender flowers. Place them in a 14fl oz (400ml) jar—they should fill it about halfway. Top off with the oil, leaving a ½in (1cm) space at the top of the jar. Let infuse for 30 days.

Prepare the salve After 30 days, strain the lavender oil to remove the flowers, then pour the oil into a heatproof bowl set over a pan of barely simmering water. Add the soy wax or beeswax and stir to melt together. Carefully pour the mixture into your chosen containers and let cool until completely solid.

Storage Store in a cool, dry place. This salve will keep for several months.

Note

» It's important to note that while lavender can be beneficial for many, it might cause allergic reactions in some individuals. It's always advisable to do a patch test before using any new skincare product extensively.

Hand Soap

These DIY natural hand soaps are the perfect way to save money while creating a fully natural product for cleansing the largest organ of the human body—our skin. We use a soap base, which you can buy inexpensively online. In total, you spend only a small amount to make a year's supply! You can use lots of different combinations of fragrances, including things growing in your own garden.

Makes 12

Prep time 25 minutes

Ingredients

Chocolate and coffee
1lb 2oz (500g) soap base, cut into
 small pieces
½ tsp ground coffee
½ tsp cocoa powder
2 tbsp vitamin E oil
10 drops vanilla essential oil
 (optional)

Calendula and lemon
1lb 2oz (500g) soap base, cut into
 small pieces
2 tbsp grated shea butter
1 tbsp dry calendula petals
20 drops lemon essential oil or
 calendula oil

Lavender and oats
1lb 2oz (500g) soap base, cut into
 small pieces
2 tbsp rolled oats
20 drops lavender essential oil
2 tbsp dried lavender flowers

Orange and rosemary
1lb 2oz (500g) soap base, cut into
 small pieces
½ tbsp finely chopped dried
 rosemary
10 drops orange essential oil
10 drops rosemary essential oil
dried orange zest (optional)

Equipment
silicone soap molds

- -

Melt the soap base Melt the soap base in a heatproof bowl set over a pan of barely simmering water.

Mix Once the base is melted, turn off the heat and stir in the oils and other ingredients and mix well. If you're making the chocolate and coffee soap, mix the coffee and cocoa powder with the vitamin E oil before adding it to the soap base.

Pour and set Pour the soap mixture into the silicone molds and let set. This will take 30–50 minutes.

Storage Store in a cool, dry place. The soaps will keep for several months.

Notes
» If you are using a powder (as for the chocolate and coffee), make sure to mix the powders thoroughly with your oil before you combine with the melted soap base to eliminate clumps.
» If using shea butter, ensure it's grated, not chopped, as it takes longer to melt than the soap base.
» Be aware that any ingredients you add or change can make the mixture harder or less oily, or may make it solidify faster.

Chop

Melt

Mix

Set

Mint Lip Balm

In this simple recipe, herbs are combined with a few other ingredients to create an effective lip balm that is chemical-free and much more in line with the natural needs of your skin. And the best thing? It's extremely cheap, yet makes a special gift for any friends or family. I normally source free raw beeswax from local farmers, but you can also source it online.

Makes 24 lip balms

Prep time 5 minutes

Cooking time 2 hours, plus cooling time

Ingredients

3½oz (100g) mint or lemon balm, finely chopped

6½ tbsp (100ml) olive oil

beeswax (1:3 ratio to the infused oil; if you prefer, you can use soy wax)

10 drops vitamin E oil

a few drops of peppermint essential oil (optional)

Equipment

24 × 15ml lip balm containers

Infuse the oil Combine the herbs and olive oil in a small heatproof bowl set over a pan of barely simmering water. Infuse for 2 hours, ensuring it simmers rather than boils.

Strain and separate oil Strain the mixture through a piece of muslin. Let the strained oil rest for at least 4 hours or overnight to allow any liquid to separate from the oil.

Make the lip balm mixture Measure the separated oil into a small heatproof bowl. Add grated beeswax in a 1:3 ratio to the oil. Place the bowl over a pan of barely simmering water and stir until the wax melts into the oil. Take off the heat and let cool for a few minutes, then add the vitamin E oil and peppermint essential oil (if using). Mix well.

Transfer to containers Pour the mixture into the containers and let cool and solidify—this will take about 20–30 minutes.

Storage Store in a cool, dry place. Shelf life can vary, but typically these lip balms will last for several months.

Eucalyptus Shower Steamers

I have to confess, I'm a fan of long baths with candles and bath bombs—sometimes I even work from the bath! However, not everyone has a bath, so we've created these shower steamers. They're the perfect trick to fight a cold or simply relax after a long day at work. They are fully natural and extremely easy to make.

Makes 15–20

Prep time 15–20 minutes, plus
   drying time

Ingredients

1 cup (140g) baking soda

½ cup (65g) citric acid

½ cup (65g) cornstarch

60 drops eucalyptus essential oil

½ tsp spirulina powder

2–3 tsp dried lavender flowers

Equipment

small spray bottle filled with a
   50:50 mix of water and vodka
   or rubbing alcohol

1–2 cupcake pans

Mix In a large bowl, mix together the baking soda, citric acid and cornstarch. Add the eucalyptus oil, spirulina and lavender, and stir to combine. Spray lightly with the water and vodka or rubbing alcohol to moisten. Test the mixture by squeezing it with your hands—if it holds its shape, it's good to go. If not, spray again.

Mold Press the mixture into the cupcake molds and leave overnight to dry completely.

Storage Store in an airtight container in a cool, dry place. Use within a few months for best results. To use the steamers, simply place them on the floor of the shower cubicle or bath tub as you shower and enjoy the aromas.

~~~~~~~~~~

Note

» You can get creative with this recipe and add your favorite oils and herbs to create your own scent combinations. For a truly spalike experience, we usually hang a eucalyptus stem in the shower too.

Index

A

almond flour: whole orange almond cake 146

almond milk: cocoa peanut butter cereal 174

almonds
  almond milk 80
  almond pulp amaretti cookies 79
  candied chocolate orange peel 144
  date bites 153
  zucchini quiche 169

amaranth 57
  popped amaranth chocolate bark 56
  stuffed zucchini 113

amaranth leaf dal 58

amaretti cookies, almond pulp 79

amaretto liqueur: almond pulp amaretti cookies 79

apple juice: apple kombucha 130

apples
  apple strudel 132
  green tomato chutney 122
  red cabbage soup 23

aquafaba
  almond pulp amaretti cookies 79
  chickpea chocolate mousse 71
  vegetable pasta dough 162

arancini 62

arrabbiata sauce, vegan 49

avocados: stuffed lettuce leaves 22

B

baking soda: shower steamers 184

baklava, hazelnut pulp and chocolate 76

bark, popped amaranth chocolate 56

basil: green tomato chutney 122

beans: feijoada 67

beeswax: lip balm 183

beets
  beet focaccia 165–67
  lacto-fermented vegetables 32
  rainbow falafel 68
  vegetable skin powders 34

berries, refrigerating 10

best-by dates 9

black beans: feijoada 67

black pepper: curry powder mix 44

black sesame seed butter 84

blondies, pistachio 82

bread crumbs 172

breads
  beet focaccia 165–67
  bread crumbs 172
  croutons 172
  rice bread 64
  sourdough breads 172
  sourdough starter 170
  stuffed flatbread 47
  using up stale bread 172

broccoli: lacto-fermented vegetables 32

butter beans: red cabbage soup 23

buttercream: poppy seed flower-fetti cake 105

butterfly pea flowers: purple lemonade 143

butternut squash: rainbow falafel 68

butters, plant-based
  black sesame seed butter 84
  herb butter 156
  nasturtium butter 96
  pumpkin seed butter 87
  sunflower butter 87–91

C

cabbage
  kimchi 29
  red cabbage soup 23
  sarmale de post 24–27

cakes
  carrot cupcakes 43
  pistachio blondies 82
  poppy seed flower-fetti cake 105
  whole orange almond cake 146

calendula
  calendula and lemon hand soap 180
  calendula-infused oil 104
  drying calendula 104

candied chocolate orange peel 144

cannelloni crêpes, spinach and ricotta 18

carrot-top pesto 42

carrots
  arancini 62
  carrot cupcakes 43
  carrot Turkish truffles 42
  crispy potato and carrot skin snacks 40
  fresh carrot juice 40
  ginger shot 44
  kimchi 29
  lacto-fermented vegetables 32
  vegetable skin powders 34

cashews
  carrot cupcakes 43
  plant-based ricotta 164
  tiramisu 81

cauliflower
  lacto-fermented vegetables 32
  sticky cauliflower wings 53

cayenne powder: curry powder mix 44

cereal, cocoa peanut butter 174

cheese, plant-based
  arancini 62
  eggplant Parmigiana 118
  stuffed flatbread 47
  upside-down onion tart 38
  see also ricotta cheese

chia seeds: fruit leather 133–35

chickpeas
  chickpea chocolate mousse 71
  rainbow falafel 68

chiles: vegan arrabbiata sauce 49

chocolate
  candied chocolate orange peel 144
  chickpea chocolate mousse 71
  chocolate and coffee hand soap 180
  cocoa peanut butter cereal 174
  date bites 153
  hazelnut pulp and chocolate baklava 76
  popped amaranth chocolate bark 56

chutney
  green tomato chutney 122
  pineapple chutney 137

cloves: pineapple tepache 138

cocoa peanut butter cereal 174

coconut, shredded
  carrot cupcakes 43
  carrot Turkish truffles 42

coconut cream: carrot cupcakes 43

coconut milk: fig leaf panna cotta 149

coffee
  chocolate and coffee hand soap 180
  date seed coffee 153
  tiramisu 81

confit garlic with garden herbs 39

cookies, almond pulp amaretti 79

cordial, elderflower 99

corn
  corn cobs as fire lighters 124
  corn pancakes 128

corn cob silks: corn silk tea 129

corn cob silks: corn silk tea 129

crackers, sourdough discard 173

cream, plant-based: plant-based garlic cream 22

cream cheese, plant-based: nettle risotto 19
creativity 13
crêpes
  red lentil crêpes 72
  spinach and ricotta cannelloni crêpes 18
crispy potato and carrot skin snacks 40
croutons 172
cucumber
  cucumber juice mocktail 117
  lacto-fermented vegetables 32
  tzatziki 117
cupcakes, carrot 43
curry powder mix 44

D

dal, amaranth leaf 58
dandelion honey 106–109
dates
  date bites 153
  date seed coffee 153
dips
  eggplant dip 120
  tzatziki 117
dried goods, storing 9
drinks
  almond milk 80
  apple kombucha 130
  cucumber juice mocktail 117
  date seed coffee 153
  elderflower and mint mocktail 99
  elderflower cordial 99
  fresh carrot juice 40
  ginger bug 44
  ginger shot 44
  ginger soda 45
  hazelnut milk 76
  oat milk 60
  pineapple tepache 138
  pistachio milk 82
  purple lemonade 143
dumplings, plum 148

E

eggplants
  eggplant dip 120
  eggplant Parmigiana 118
elderberry syrup 97
elderflowers
  elderflower and mint mocktail 99
  elderflower cordial 99
eucalyptus essential oil: shower steamers
  184

F

falafel, rainbow 68
farmers' markets 13
feijoada 67
fennel seeds: curry powder mix 44
fenugreek seeds: curry powder mix 44
ferments
  apple kombucha 130
  ginger bug 44
  ginger soda 45
  kimchi 29
  lacto-fermented vegetables 32
  pineapple tepache 138
  sarmale de post 24–27
fig leaf panna cotta 149
figs
  green fig syrup 150
  stuffed figs 150
flatbread, stuffed 47
flour-based recipes 160–75
  beet focaccia 165–67
  cocoa peanut butter cereal 174
  plant-based ricotta 164
  simple pasta sauce 164
  sourdough bread 172
  sourdough discard crackers 173
  sourdough starter 170
  vegetable pasta dough 162
  zucchini quiche 169
flowers 92–109
  calendula-infused oil 104
  dandelion honey 106–109
  elderberry syrup 97
  elderflower cordial 99
  lavender-infused oil 102
  nasturtium butter 96
  nasturtium vellutata 94
  pickled nasturtium seeds 96
  poppy seed flower-fetti cake 105
  rose and raspberry granita 100
  rose powder 100
focaccia, beet 165–67
food
  food storage 9–13
  wrapping 10
freezers 13
fritters, potato 50
frosting: carrot cupcakes 43
fruit 110–53
  apple kombucha 130–31
  apple strudel 132

candied chocolate orange peel 144
corn pancakes 128
corn silk tea 129
cucumber juice mocktail 117
date bites 153
date seed coffee 153
deep-fried zucchiniflowers 114
dehydrated strawberries 139
eggplant parmigiana 118
fig leaf panna cotta 149
fruit leather 133–35
găluște cu prune 148
green fig syrup 150
green tomato chutney 122
grilled polenta with sage 124–27
leaves and stems pesto 114
pineapple chutney 137
pineapple tepache 138
preserved lemon peel 143
purple lemonade 143
salata de vinete 120
storing fruit 10
strawberry cheong 140
stuffed figs 150
stuffed zucchini 113
tomato skin powder 121
tzatziki 117
whole orange almond cake 146
see also individual types of fruit

G

găluște cu prune 148
garlic
  amaranth leaf dal 58
  beet focaccia 165–67
  confit garlic with garden herbs 39
  feijoada 67
  green tomato chutney 122
  kimchi 29
  pineapple chutney 137
  plant-based garlic cream 22
  rainbow falafel 68
  storing 10
  stuffed flatbread 47
  stuffed zucchini 113
  tzatziki 117
  vegan arrabbiata sauce 49
  vegetable skin powders 34
ginger
  curry powder mix 44
  ginger bug 44
  ginger shot 44

ginger soda 45
green tomato chutney 122
pineapple chutney 137
ginger bug 44
ginger soda 45
grains and pulses 54–73
amaranth leaf dal 58
arancini 62
chickpea chocolate mousse 71
feijoada 67
oat milk 60
oat pulp granola 61
popped amaranth chocolate bark 56
rainbow falafel 68
red lentil crêpes 72
rice bread 64
see also individual types of pulses and grains
granita, rose and raspberry 100
granola, oat pulp 61
green beans: lacto-fermented vegetables 32
green fig syrup 150
green onions: kimchi 29
green tomato chutney 122
ground "meat," plant-based: arancini 62

H

hand soap 180
hazelnuts
hazelnut milk 76
hazelnut pulp and chocolate baklava 76
herbs 154–59
confit garlic with garden herbs 39
herb bomb 156
herb butter 156
herb salt 156
mixed herbs 156
rainbow falafel 68
red lentil crêpes 72
refrigerating herbs 10
tzatziki 117
home remedies 176–85
hand soap 180
lavender skin salve 178
lip balm 183
shower steamers 184
honey, dandelion 106–109
hot pepper flakes (gochugaru): kimchi 29

J

jars
repurposing 8–9
sterilizing 8
juice, fresh carrot 40

K

kimchi 29
kombucha
apple kombucha 130
teas to avoid 131
teas to use for 131

L

lacto-fermented vegetables 32
lavender
drying lavender 102
lavender and oat hand soap 180
lavender-infused oil 102
lavender skin salve 178
shower steamers 184
leafy greens 16–29
kimchi 29
lettuce and potato soup 20
nettle risotto 19
red cabbage soup 23
refrigerating leafy greens 10
sarmale de post 24–27
spinach and ricotta cannelloni crêpes 18
stuffed lettuce leaves 22
leather, fruit 133–35
leaves and stems pesto 114
lemon balm: lip balm 183
lemonade, purple 143
lemons
calendula and lemon hand soap 180
elderflower cordial 99
poppy seed flower-fetti cake 105
preserved lemon peel 143
purple lemonade 143
strawberry cheong 140
lentils
amaranth leaf dal 58
red lentil crêpes 72
lettuce
lettuce and potato soup 20
stuffed lettuce leaves 22
lime juice: cucumber juice mocktail 117
lip balm 183
low-waste shopping 13
low-waste stores 13

M

maple syrup
hazelnut pulp and chocolate baklava 76
oat pulp granola 61
pistachio blondies 82
sticky cauliflower wings 53
upside-down onion tart 38
markets, farmers' 13
milks, plant-based
almond milk 80
hazelnut milk 76
oat milk 60
pistachio milk 82
mint
cucumber juice mocktail 117
elderflower and mint mocktail 99
lip balm 183
mocktails
cucumber juice mocktail 117
elderflower and mint mocktail 99
mousse, chickpea chocolate 71
mozzarella, plant-based: eggplant Parmigiana 118
mushrooms: sarmale de post 24–27
mustard seeds
curry powder mix 44
homemade mustard 86

N

napa cabbages: kimchi 29
nasturtium flowers 94
nasturtium leaves
nasturtium butter 96
nasturtium vellutata 94
nasturtium seeds, pickled 96
nettle risotto 19
noodles, potato 48
nuts and seeds 74–91
almond milk 80
almond pulp amaretti cookies 79
black sesame seed butter 84
hazelnut milk 76
hazelnut pulp and chocolate baklava 76
homemade mustard 86
oat pulp granola 61
pistachio blondies 82
pistachio milk 82
sunflower butter 87–91
tiramisu 81
see also individual types of nuts and seeds

O

oat cream: nasturtium vellutata 94
oats
    lavender and oat hand soap 180
    oat milk 60
    oat pulp granola 61
oils
    calendula-infused oil 104
    lavender-infused oil 102
olive oil: lip balm 183
onions
    lacto-fermented vegetables 32
    sarmale de post 24–27
    storing 10
    upside-down onion tart 38
    vegetable skin powders 34
oranges
    candied chocolate orange peel 144
    ginger shot 44
    green tomato chutney 122
    orange and rosemary hand soap 180
    pineapple chutney 137
    whole orange almond cake 146

P

pancakes, corn 128
panna cotta, fig leaf 149
pantries, ingredients 9
Parmigiana, eggplant 118
parsley: salata de vinete 120
pasta
    simple pasta sauce 164
    spinach and ricotta cannelloni crêpes 18
    vegetable pasta dough 162
peanut butter: cocoa peanut butter
    cereal 174
peas
    arancini 62
    stuffed zucchini 113
peppers: lacto-fermented vegetables 32
pesto
    carrot-top pesto 42
    leaves and stems pesto 114
phyllo pastry: hazelnut pulp and chocolate
    baklava 76
pickled nasturtium seeds 96
pine nuts
    carrot-top pesto 42
    leaves and stems pesto 114
pineapple
    pineapple chutney 137

pineapple tepache 138
pistachios
    carrot Turkish truffles 42
    date bites 153
    pistachio blondies 82
    pistachio milk 82
plum dumplings 148
polenta: grilled polenta with sage 124–27
popped amaranth chocolate bark 56
poppy seed flower-fetti cake 105
potatoes
    crispy potato and carrot skin snacks 40
    lettuce and potato soup 20
    plum dumplings 148
    potato fritters 50
    potato noodles 48
    rainbow falafel 68
    storing 10
    stuffed flatbread 47
powders
    curry powder mix 44
    rose powder 100
    strawberry powder 139
    tomato skin powder 121
    vegetable skin powders 34
preserved lemon peel 143
puff pastry, plant-based
    apple strudel 132
    upside-down onion tart 38
puffed quinoa: oat pulp granola 61
pulses and grains 54–73
    amaranth leaf dal 58
    arancini 62
    chickpea chocolate mousse 71
    feijoada 67
    oat milk 60
    oat pulp granola 61
    popped amaranth chocolate bark 56
    rainbow falafel 68
    red lentil crêpes 72
    rice bread 64
    see also individual types of pulses and
    grains
pumpkin seed butter 87
purple lemonade 143

Q

quiche, zucchini 169
quinoa: stuffed zucchini 113
quinoa, puffed: oat pulp granola 61

R

radishes
    kimchi 29
    lacto-fermented vegetables 32
rainbow falafel 68
raspberry juice: rose and raspberry granita
    100
red cabbage soup 23
refill stores 13
refrigerating food 9
rice
    arancini 62
    nettle risotto 19
    rice bread 64
    sarmale de post 24–27
    stuffed lettuce leaves 22
    using leftover rice 62
ricotta, plant-based 164
    deep-fried zucchini flowers 114
    spinach and ricotta cannelloni crêpes 18
    stuffed figs 150
risotto, nettle 19
roots and shoots 30–53
    carrot cupcakes 43
    carrot-top pesto 42
    confit garlic with garden herbs 39
    crispy potato and carrot skin snacks 40
    curry powder mix 44
    fresh carrot juice 41
    ginger bug 44
    ginger shot 44
    ginger soda 45
    lacto-fermented vegetables 32
    potato fritters 50
    potato noodles 48
    refrigerating root vegetables 10
    sticky cauliflower wings 53
    stuffed flatbread 47
    upside-down onion tart 38
    vegan arrabbiata sauce 49
    vegetable skin powders 34
rose petals
    rose and raspberry granita 100
    rose powder 100
rosemary
    confit garlic with garden herbs 39
    orange and rosemary hand soap 180

S

sage, grilled polenta with 124–27
salata de vinete 120
salt, herb 156
sarmale de post 24–27
sausages, plant-based: feijoada 67
SCOBY 130
seeds and nuts 74–91
  almond milk 80
  almond pulp amaretti cookies 79
  black sesame seed butter 84
  hazelnut milk 76
  hazelnut pulp and chocolate baklava 76
  homemade mustard 86
  oat pulp granola 61
  pistachio blondies 82
  pistachio milk 82
  sunflower butter 87–91
  tiramisu 81
  see also individual types of nuts
    and seeds
sesame seeds: black sesame seed butter 84
shopping, low-waste 13
shots, ginger 44
shower steamers 184
simple syrup 117
skin salve, lavender 178
soaps
  calendula and lemon hand soap 180
  chocolate and coffee hand soap 180
  hand soap 180
  lavender and oat hand soap 180
  orange and rosemary hand soap 180
soda, ginger 45
soups
  lettuce and potato soup 20
  nasturtium vellutata 94
  red cabbage soup 23
sourdough
  sourdough breads 172
  sourdough discard crackers 173
  sourdough starter 170
soy milk: poppy seed flower-fetti cake 105
spice mix: curry powder mix 44
spinach
  rainbow falafel 68
  spinach and ricotta cannelloni crêpes 18
split red lentils
  amaranth leaf dal 58
  red lentil crêpes 72
squash: rainbow falafel 68

stem vegetables, refrigerating 9–10
sticky cauliflower wings 53
storage, food 9–13
  best-by dates 9
  freezing food 13
  pantry 9
  refrigerating food 9–10
  storing at room temperature 10
  wrapping food 10
stores, refill or low-waste 13
strawberries
  dehydrated strawberries 139
  strawberry cheong 140
  strawberry powder 139
strudel, apple 132
stuffed cabbage rolls 24–27
stuffed figs 150
stuffed flatbread 47
stuffed lettuce leaves 22
stuffed zucchini 113
sunflower oil: lavender skin salve 178
sunflower seeds
  oat pulp granola 61
  sunflower butter 87–91
sweet corn: stuffed lettuce leaves 22
syrups
  elderberry syrup 97
  green fig syrup 150
  simple syrup 117
  strawberry cheong 140

T

tahini 84
tart, upside-down onion 38
teas
  apple kombucha 130
  corn silk tea 129
  teas to use for kombucha 131
tempura batter: deep-fried zucchini
    flowers 114
tepache, pineapple 138
Thai basil: green tomato chutney 122
thyme: confit garlic with garden herbs 39
tiramisu 81
tofu
  tiramisu 81
  zucchini quiche 169
tomatoes
  arancini 62
  eggplant Parmigiana 118
  green tomato chutney 122
  sarmale de post 24–27

simple pasta sauce 164
spinach and ricotta cannelloni crêpes 18
storing 10
stuffed flatbread 47
tomato skin powder 121
vegan arrabbiata sauce 49
truffles, carrot Turkish 42
turmeric
  curry powder mix 44
  ginger shot 44
tzatziki 117

U

upside-down onion tart 38
use-by dates 9

V

vegan arrabbiata sauce 49
vegetable skins
  crispy potato and carrot skin snacks 40
  vegetable skin powders 34
vegetables
  lacto-fermented vegetables 32
  refrigerating 9–10
  vegetable pasta dough 162
  see also individual types of vegetables
vellutata, nasturtium 94
vitamin E oil: lip balm 183

W

walnuts: stuffed figs 150
wax wraps 10
wrapping food 10

Y

yogurt, plant-based
  carrot cupcakes 43
  stuffed flatbread 47
  tzatziki 117

Z

zucchini
  zucchini quiche 169
  nasturtium vellutata 94
  stuffed zucchini 113
zucchini flowers, deep-fried 114
zucchini leaves and stems: leaves and
    stems pesto 114

Author's Acknowledgments

Writing *Low Waste Kitchen* has been an incredible journey, and there are many people who have supported and inspired me along the way.

First, I want to express my deepest gratitude to my partner, Iasmina, who has been with me throughout every step of this adventure. From experimenting with recipes in our small London flat to sharing ideas for reducing waste, your unwavering support, patience, and belief in this project have meant everything to me.

I am also forever grateful to my grandparents, Pietro and Ruth, whose values and traditions shaped the heart of this book. Their wisdom taught me the importance of cherishing every resource and living in harmony with nature. This book is a tribute to them and the way they lived, and I hope it inspires others as much as they inspired me.

To my family, Paolo, Katia, and Anna, thank you for encouraging me to carry on with this journey and for supporting me in everything I've done. A special note of gratitude to my dad, who, despite suffering an accident, never let it dampen his spirit or strength. His resilience and unwavering determination have been a guiding force in my life, teaching me to never give up, no matter the challenges I face.

A heartfelt thank you to my friends and the wider community who have stood by me, offering encouragement and valuable feedback throughout this process. Your shared meals, conversations, and enthusiasm have helped keep my passion alive.

I'd also like to thank my community on social media, especially those who followed along as I shared tips, recipes, and sustainable living ideas. Your engagement and feedback have helped me grow and evolve, and this book wouldn't be the same without your support.

Finally, a big thank you to my editor and publishing team for believing in this project and helping bring it to life. Your guidance has been invaluable in shaping this book into something I'm truly proud of.

To everyone who's been a part of this journey, I'm deeply thankful. This book wouldn't exist without you, and I hope it brings value to those who read it, just as it's brought joy and purpose to my life.

About the Author

Alessandro Vitale (aka @SpicyMoustache) has captivated a vast audience across YouTube, Instagram, and Tiktok with his fast-paced, easy-to-follow, low-waste videos. Originally learning about growing and preserving food with his grandparents in his native Italy, Alessandro has always connected to the land and food cultivation. He moved to London in 2016, establishing himself as an urban gardener with his first book, *Rebel Gardening* (Watkins, 2023) which focuses on urban growing. Alessandro has appeared on *Gardener's World* and *Tamron Hall*, and has featured in *The Times* and *The Guardian*. He regularly collaborates with influencers and sustainability experts, including the likes of FAO, Epic Gardening, Gaz Oakley, and fellow DK author Ben Newell.

~~~~~~~~~~

Publisher's Acknowledgments

DK would like to thank Kate Reeves-Brown for proofreading, John Tullock for his help consulting on the US edition, and Vanessa Bird for providing the index. Thanks also to Faye Wears for additional prop styling, to Sasha Burdian, Ciara Banks, Jack Storer, and Luke Godden for photography assistance, and to Maisie Chandler for food styling assistance.

DK LONDON
Editorial Director Cara Armstrong
Senior Editor Lucy Sienkowska
Senior Designer Barbara Zuniga
Production Editor David Almond
US Senior Editor Jennette ElNaggar
Senior Production Controller Samantha Cross
DTP and Design Coordinator Heather Blagden
Sales Material and Jackets Coordinator Emily Cannings
Art Director Maxine Pedliham

Editorial Tara O'Sullivan
Photography Art Direction and Design Sarah Snelling
Jacket Design George Saad
Design Development Luke Bird
Photography Robert Billington
Prop Styling Daisy Shayler-Webb
Food Styling Flossy McAslan

First American Edition, 2025
Published in the United States by
DK RED, an imprint of DK Publishing,
a division of Penguin Random House LLC
1745 Broadway, 20th Floor, New York, NY 10019

A catalog record for this book
is available from the Library of Congress.
ISBN 978-0-5939-6111-7

DK books are available at special discounts when purchased
in bulk for sales promotions, premiums, fund-raising,
or educational use. For details, contact: DK Publishing Special Markets,
1745 Broadway, 20th Floor, New York, NY 10019
SpecialSales@dk.com

Printed and bound in Slovakia
www.dk.com

MIX
Paper | Supporting
responsible forestry
FSC™ C018179

This book was made with Forest
Stewardship Council™ certified
paper—one small step in DK's
commitment to a sustainable future.
**Learn more at www.dk.com/uk/
information/sustainability**